LIVING WELL
WITH STRESS

Psychological Guidance and
Consultation Service,
University of Montreal

LIVING WELL
WITH STRESS

Self-management guide

francine boucher
andré binette

Published by :
Editions de Mortagne
250, Industrial Boulevard
Boucherville (Quebec)
J4B 2X4
Tél. : (514) 641-2387

Consulting Publisher :
S.O.C.P.
2101, Edouard Montpetit Boulevard
Montreal, Quebec
H3C 3J7

Translation :
Blanche Hodder

Cover Illustration :
Clic Communications

Legal deposit :
National Library of Canada
National Library of Quebec
October 1989

ISBN : 2-89074-905-3

1 2 3 4 - 89 - 92 91 90 89

Printed in Canada

This program has been created by the Psychological Guidance and Consultation Service of the University of Montreal.

The Psychological Guidance and Consultation Service of the University of Montreal, with eleven psychologists who are members of recognized professional associations, offers University students and staff, as well as the general public, a complete range of psychological services.

S.O.C.P.
2101, Edouard Montpetit Boulevard
Montreal, Quebec
H3C 3J7

TABLE OF CONTENTS

INTRODUCTION

The term "stress" is used a lot nowadays. We talk about stress as an explanatory factor in numerous personal or social problems. Every day, new solutions are proposed for exorcising this demon of modern life. In this high-tech age, there is even a pocket apparatus on the market, the GSR-2, which lets us take our own blood pressure and then do whatever is necessary when the readout shows a critical level. Do we really need to inflate the profits of the company that sells GSR-2 or can we use our own inner resources to deal with the problem?

After all, what is stress but an innate response of the body, a mechanism for adapting and surviving? As such, the stress response is necessary and inevitable. However, if this response is constantly triggered and surpasses the adaptive limits of the human body, illness, even death, may follow.

Although we cannot avoid stress, we can, nonetheless, learn to use it to our advantage rather than to our detriment. The purpose of this guide is to suggest the most appropriate methods of doing this.

A metastrategy can be derived from the strategies proposed: the ability to solve a problem. In fact, self-management of stress implies a problem-solving approach, i.e. defining the problem in real terms, listing and choosing strategies for solving it, effectively applying these strategies and, finally, verifying their suitability and usefulness by trying them out.

To help you define the problem, the first part of the guide will deal with the nature of stress, types of stress factors and the main distress symptoms. The second part of the guide will take up stress management. First, some exercises will be suggested for identifying the stressful situations in your life. Then we will present the most appropriate strategies for solving these problems, either managing external stress factors or managing internal resistance to stress. You will then have to choose a solution and apply it.

The third part of the guide offers five important strategies in stress management. Interested readers will find useful information on time management, physical exercise, diet, relaxation methods and emotional control.

You can read this book at one sitting but, in all probability, you will gain little from it. To self-manage stress, you must not only be well-acquainted with the subject but also adopt the appropriate change strategy or strategies. Do we need to emphasize that the exercises should be practised? It's up to you to decide.

I

KNOWING
WHAT STRESS IS

1. A brief background

Although there's a lot of talk about stress nowadays, research in the field is relatively recent.

Of course, during the second half of the 19th century, Claude Bernard had already pointed out that a fixed internal environment is the underlying condition of a free and independent life. Every living animal tends to maintain a state of internal stability in spite of changes in the external environment. Around 50 years later, Walter Cannon gave this physiological phenomenon a name: homeostasis. He concluded from his work that animals or primitive men, when confronted by danger to their internal equilibrium, would either prepare to fight or take flight. In a now-classic study, he attributed the deaths of voodoo victims to their difficulties in using the fight-or-flight mechanism to reestablish their homeostasis. According to him, the belief of these people that spells or curses could be fatal, a belief strengthened by their society, provoked such a state of terror that their adrenal medullas were overstimulated, causing death through a completely natural process.

But it took the work of Hans Selye to provide a clearer understanding of the stress phenomenon. In 1936, Selye noticed that toxic glandular preparations injected into animals produced a stereotyped syndrome characterized by hypertrophy and hyperactivity of the cortex of the adrenal glands, atrophy of the thymus and lymph glands and the appearance of gastrointestinal ulcers. He also noted that various factors (chills, traumas, infections) caused the same symptoms. He first called the phenomenon "syndrome produced by various nocuous agents." He then described it as a general adaptation syndrome or biological stress syndrome (and, in 1950, he introduced the term "stress" into French scientific literature.)

2. The many definitions of stress

Today, we are still far from a unanimous definition of the term "stress". We can distinguish three different viewpoints when examining the multiple definitions given by researchers. Some authors approach stress from the "physiological response" angle, that is, the group of biochemical changes which typically occur in the organism when the internal equilibrium is threatened. Other authors use the term "stress" to describe emotional or behavioral responses to a stress condition. They describe the emotions provoked during stress as well as the behavioral changes observed. Other authors use the term "stress" to talk of a stimulus. They report events, situations and sources of stress for the human being.

PHYSIOLOGICAL REACTIONS

Stress is characterized by a group of stereotyped physiological reactions which can be observed and measured in the laboratory. These biochemical reactions may be benign, but in some cases they alter the body's functioning to the point of inducing illness and death.

Some physiological reactions to stress are well known: the heart rate increases, muscles contract and respiration accelerates. But these reactions are only a minute part of all the biochemical changes triggered by a stress condition. The stress reaction is highly complex. To explain it further, we must look at a certain amount of technological data, some of it difficult to assimilate but necessary to understanding the phenomenon.

Selye defines stress as the body's non-specific response to any demand made on it. Various environmental stimuli — cold, heat or noise — produce specific effects in the body. Cold makes us shiver, heat makes us sweat and noise produces auditory sensations. What Selye has shown is that apart from these specific reactions, stressful conditions all produce an identical non-specific biological response that he calls stress. This biological response is a non-specific intensification needed to bring about adaptive functions and, through these, reestablish normalcy.

The three phases of the general adaptation syndrome describe the non-specific stress reaction (seeFigure 1). At its first exposure to the stress agent, the body is immediately put into a state of alert by a set of biochemical changes whose goal is to permit flight or fight and, ultimately, reestablish internal equilibrium. Simultaneously, the body's resistance decreases and if the stress agent is too intense, death may follow. The alarm reaction is followed by a resistance phase if exposure to the stressor is compatible with adaptation. The characteristic reactions of the first phase continue but are more adapted to the need for defence. The body's resistance rises above normal. This second phase continues until healing occurs or, if the organism is no longer capable of maintaining its adaptive state, an exhaustion phase ends the process. The signs of the alarm reaction reappear and organic injury or death eventually occurs. When an autopsy is performed on an animal that dies of stress, atrophy of the adrenal glands, lymphoid tissue and thymus gland and gastrointestinal ulcers are found.

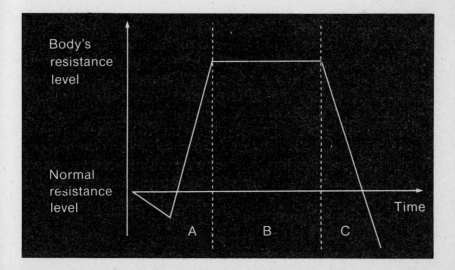

Figure 1 : Selye's three phases of the general adaptation syndrome.

The sequence of the three phases of the general adaptation syndrome is invariable but the process may not be completed if the stressor's action ceases. The duration of the these three phases depends on the body's ability to adapt and the intensity of the stressor.

Whether the stress agent be physical, physiological or emotional, the principal response pathways to stress agents are the same (see Figure 2). The danger message is first transmitted to the hypothalamus, a part of the brain at the base of the skull. The hypothalamus activates the autonomic nervous system and the pituitary gland, also located in the cranium. Under this influence, the pituitary gland secretes hormones, principally ACTH (adrenocorticotropic hormone). This hormone acts on the outer covering (cortex) of the adrenal glands, which are located just above the kidneys. In turn, the adrenal glands secrete the corticoids involved in inflammatory and anti-inflammatory processes. Over-production of ACTH and hyperactivity of the adrenal cortex are among

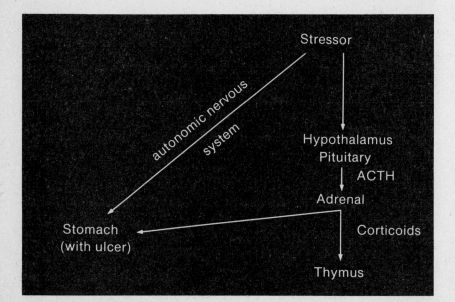

Figure 2: Principal response pathways to stressors, according to Selye.

the principal characteristics of the stereotyped adaptation syndrome. The intensity of stress can be measured in the laboratory from the levels of corticoids found in the blood.

The autonomic nervous system makes many physical changes. Several muscles contract and dilate the blood vessels to speed up blood circulation. Cardiac rhythm accelerates. Respiration becomes more rapid and arterial tension rises. Subcutaneous blood vessels contract, sometimes causing a sudden pallor. Digestive activity is inhibited and perception sharpens to identify the danger better. These changes in body functioning can elicit ulcer production in the stomach and intestine.

The pituitary also activates the adrenal medullas (the internal parts of the adrenal glands) which then secrete other hormones characteristic of stress called catecholamines — adrenaline and noradrenaline. This hormonal triggering is what causes the sensation of feverishness and exuberance mingled with distress so often associated with emotional stress reactions. The effect of catecholamines is multiple : they stimulate oxygen consumption and basal metabolism. They trigger production of a larger number of red and white blood cells and facilitate blood clotting. To increase available energy, they also activate adipose tissue to release fatty acids and stimulate the liver to produce more sugar.

All the changes brought about by the action of the autonomic nervous system and the pituitary gland are aimed at immediate mobilization of the body's resources and better adaptation. Senses are sharpened in order to perceive danger. Lung and heart functioning is optimized. The immune system's ability to fight wounds and infection is reinforced. The body is ready to use the available energy for vitally important tasks.

Stress is thus a group of clearly defined physiological responses to permit flight or fight in the face of danger.

EMOTIONAL AND BEHAVIORAL REACTIONS

Another way of describing stress is to explain the many emotional and behavioral reactions that it induces. Emotional and behavioral reactions to stress are often more apparent than physiological reactions since they are visible to everyone. When reacting to an internal or external stimulus which upsets the internal equilibrium, a human being laughs, cries, gets angry or trembles with fear. Under intense stress, behavior becomes more erratic or more energetic. If the stress is negative, behavioral changes may show up in an increase in the number of errors when performing a task, lowered job performance or deterioration of interpersonal relationships. The student whose mind goes blank before an exam paper or the administrator who, time after time, makes poor decisions both know the harmful effects of stress. If, on the other hand, the stress is positive, performance may noticeably improve or may increase stamina. A large number of students give a highly satisfactory performance when deadlines have them up against the wall.

Although emotional and behavioral reactions to stress are evident, they are difficult to study and measure. Emotions and behavior vary according to culture, time period, context and personality. Experiences are varied and qualified according to the situation. Thus, in social situations, certain emotions are inhibited; despite intense stress, we refrain from weeping or trembling in public because these emotions attract other people's attention. Because of these difficulties in measuring emotional and behavioral reactions, although they are reliable subjective signs of stress, researchers prefer to describe stress in terms of physiological response.

THE STIMULUS

A third criterion for defining stress is an examination of the stimuli or the agents which produce the stress reaction in the human being. But from this angle, the stress response is difficult to anticipate or to define. The stimuli which trigger the stress reaction in some individuals do not do so in others. The reactions provoked, whether physical, emotional or behavioral, differ according to the case. It would seem that with the exception of extreme, sudden life-threatening situations, there is no stimulus that is a stressor for everyone.

In the laboratory, people have been subjected to stimuli usually considered as stressors and, by minimizing the emotional factors involved, it has been demonstrated that the stress reaction does not appear or is greatly diminished. Thus, researchers will expose subjects to a loud noise, warning them when the noise will be heard or giving them a means to end the noise. Subjects then react to the noise but the non-specific stress reaction does not appear or is barely present.

This is why many researchers question Selye's thesis of the non-specific nature of the stress reaction. In other words, stress may not be triggered by all the stimuli to which we are exposed but by the action of certain psychological factors which make us perceive certain stimuli as a source of danger to the organism. A currently proposed definition of stress is a condition of the organism when it perceives that its well-being is threatened and it must use all its energies for self-protection.

This new definition of stress implies a complex interaction between stressors and the organism's response. For a stimulus to trigger a stress reaction, the organism must perceive it as a threat or a source of danger. And perception of danger depends on a number of variables. We can mention, among others, the nature and intensity of the stimulus, the cognitive expectations and evaluations, past experience, values, personality, emotional factors, the goals or the needs of each person. An examination may be stressful for one student and not for another, depending on their knowledge of the subject, their previous successes or failures, their motivation, their personality, etc. Defining stress from the stress agent thus becomes very difficult.

Despite the scope of the task, researchers have nonetheless found several general rules. First, previous experience of the stress agent (repeated exposure, coaching, preliminary information) diminishes the stress felt. However, a perceived failure in a task is a stressful experience in itself and the effects show up as decreased efficiency in subsequent performance. This rule holds true in psycho-motor tasks and in problem-solving, reasoning and learning tasks.

It has also been shown that, in general, the greater the stimulation, the greater the stress felt. Figure 3, taken from Stress without Distress, illustrates that stress increases with the emotional intensity of an experience, with little regard to its pleasant or unpleasant nature. The stress felt depends solely on the intensity of the demand for readjustment or adaptation. Note in passing that the figure is drawn according to the primary definitions of stress. The stress level is never at zero because a total absence of stress, by these definitions, is synonymous with death.

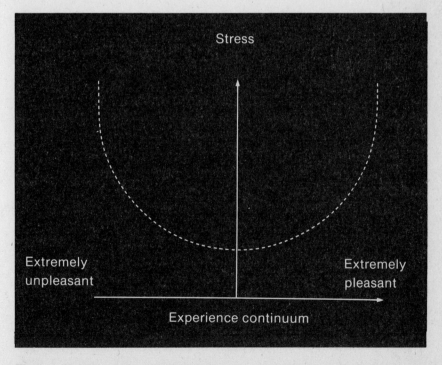

Figure 3: Theoretical model showing the relation between stress and various types of life experiences, according to Selye. (1974).

The inverted U curve (see Figure 4) illustrates the relationship between the level of stress felt and performance quality. As can be seen, performance improves when the stress felt is moderate and deteriorates when the stress felt is too high or is non-existent. In other words, when a person must face an exceptionally intense, complex, ambiguous or novel situation, the reaction is generally anxiety, a mixture of attention, curiosity and fear, which triggers an optimal performance. However, as the anxiety increases, the performance may deteriorate and more regressive defence behavior may even appear. There is hardly any doubt that sudden and intense stress or even weak but prolonged or repeated stress can exhaust the organism's adaptive energies.

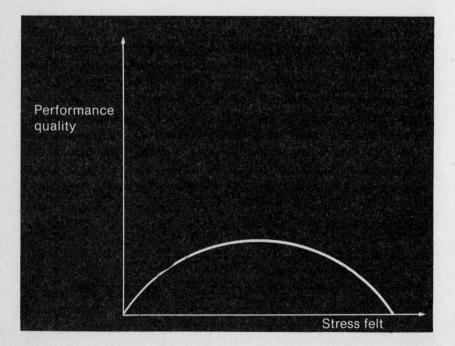

Figure 4: Relation between the level of stress felt and performance quality.

However, too low a level of stress can cause symptoms similar to those of intense stress. Isolation experiments, in the laboratory or in the natural environment, where there is sensory or perceptive deprivation or exposure to as uniform a stimulation as possible show that subjects display typical crisis symptoms : acute depression, panic, hallucinations, difficulty in perception and reasoning. The nervous system seems to need a certain degree of excitation to function optimally.

Interpersonal or social stimulation appears to follow the same law as physical stimulation. While some studies show that the presence of others or communication with others reduces the stressful effects of some physical dangers or harmful environments, other studies note that stress engendered by social or intimate relationships can be intense, as each of us has undoubtedly experienced. While social isolation may be difficult to bear, life with others is not always a rose garden.

Thus it seems that a very low level of physical or social stimulation or a too-uniform stimulation is as much a threat to the human being as a very intense, very complex, very ambiguous or very unexpected level of stimulation.

CONCLUSION

The difficulties of measuring the stress phenomenon are easily seen by examining the three criteria for defining stress. As Isabelle Trocheris has said, "stress is a word for which very few people could give a precise definition. However, in biology, stress or rather stresses have a biological reality whose excessive repetition on individuals seems to be a characteristic of our modern industrial society."

Several conditions can produce stress but reactions vary with the individual. Some people may be stressed in a situation to which others have no reaction. Furthermore, individual responses vary with the time and the context. This means that the notion of a stereotyped reaction to stress must be reevaluated. Before predicting which conditions will be stressful, the motivational structure and previous history of the persons exposed to the stress agents must be known.

In the search for a concept of stress which will unite theoreticians and researchers in the field, some people have proposed abandoning the term altogether and others propose to use it to describe a field of study and interest including stress-producing stimuli, the reactions themselves and the numerous mediating processes between the stressor and the corresponding reaction. What matters is not that the stimuli are internal or external but that they test or surpass the adaptive resources of the individual or the social system.

3. Stress agents

As we have seen, many researchers use the term stress to describe not only the organism's reactions but also the many internal and external pressures which provoke these reactions. Thus, Toffler will say that modern life is stressful because today's society creates living conditions which will shortly reach the adaptive limits of many human beings. The term stress also refers to stressors or stress agents.

DEFINITION OF A STRESS AGENT

Selye defines the stress agent as any demand made on the mind or body. This is a very global definition and avoids the thorny problems of individual differences and adaptation and learning phenomena. For example, it may be true that a noisy air conditioner will be stressful for one person; it is also possible that this stimulus will not stress someone else. Although research is not yet conclusive, it is preferable, as we have seen, to know the personality and the previous history of the person exposed to a stimulus before predicting that this stimulus will be a stress agent.

All stimuli that the organism perceives as a threat to its self-preservation or to the satisfaction of its physical or psychological needs are thus considered as stress agents. At the physical level, let's mention the need for food, sex and sleep and, at the psychological level, the need for self-esteem, accomplishment, success, power, understanding of oneself and the environment, pleasure and beauty.

Some people feel that only extremely life-threatening situations are stressful for all human beings. Individual differences would explain why some stimuli stress some individuals and only act specifically on others.

Stress agents are many and varied. They can be new or familiar, brief or lasting, internal or external, real or imaginary. They can be more or less intense. Figure 5 illustrates some examples of stressors using two of these variables, intensity and duration.

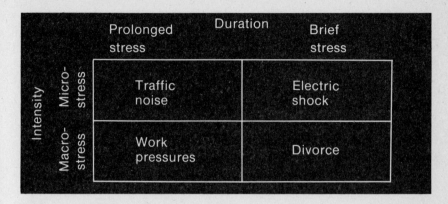

Figure 5: Some examples of stress agents using two variables, intensity and duration.

Stress agents can be "negative" or "positive," pleasant or unpleasant. Happy events in life can cause as much stress as painful ones. For example, a marriage or creative work can be as stressful as loss of a job or the death or a spouse.

An anticipated stimulus can act as a stressor. Some research has shown that the anticipation of an event may be more stressful than the event itself. For example, parachutists are often more intensely stressed before the jump than during the jump itself. The sight of a hypodermic needle can cause more terror than the injection itself.

On the other hand, an unexpected occurrence can cause even greater stress. A sudden bereavement, car accident, or horrifying sight will be more harmful than if they are expected. Research on hospital patients has shown the importance of preparatory information in reducing the stress of surgery, for example.

To help you understand the variety of stress agents to which you are exposed, let's try to classify them according to their psychological significance and their source.

CLASSIFICATION OF STRESS AGENTS

Stress agents may be classed in many ways. We are giving two classifications. Sharpe and Lewis classify stressors by their psychological significance. The International Stress Institute dwells on the nature or the source of the stress agent.

Stressors may be divided into six classes by their psychological significance: performance stress, threat stress, boredom stress, frustration stress, loss or bereavement stress and physical stress.

1. *Performance stress*

This is any stressor inherent in accomplishing physical or mental work, in the phases of planning, accomplishment, feed-back and evaluation. Also included in this group are stressors inherent in situations perceived or considered as having to conform to norms, models or standards, thus to value judgment situations such as social roles, sexual roles or self-expectations.

2. *Threat stress*

Stress resulting from situations perceived or considered as dangerous to the physical or psychological self are classed in this category. These stressors may or may not involve an objective risk to the person's physical or psychological well- being. Examples of physical threat stressors are physical aggression, sports with varying degrees of risk, and war; psychological threat stressors are social or individual situations which pose a threat to self-esteem, self-concept, satisfaction of needs for contact, warmth, acceptance and the independence-dependence balance.

3. *Boredom stress*

This class includes stressors arising from situations perceived or considered as lacking physical or mental stimulation, such as routine situations and situations where the interpersonal or social environment is not sufficiently stimulating whether at work, in sexual relationships, conversations, recreation or one's surroundings.

4. *Frustration stress*

This category refers to any stressors inherent in situations perceived or considered as undesirable but over which one has no control. Examples are no-win situations or any form of powerlessness, whether physical (illness, imprisonment), social (injustice, manipulation) or personal (interactions where you do not get what you expect from friends, colleagues, family, school,etc.). The current increase in bureaucratic procedures leads to constant stress in large cities.

5. *Loss or bereavement stress*

This is any stress resulting from the loss of a loved one or a valued thing (money, job, youth or hoped-for gratification).

6. *Physical stress*

Any stressor which can be an immediate physical assault on the person is considered as physical stress : illness, wounds, pollution, noise, temperature, lack of exercise, overeating, fasting or drugs.

The International Stress Institute classifies stressors by their nature or their source : general stressors, physical stressors, neuropsychiatric stressors, psychosocial stressors and occupational stressors. Table 1 gives a list of the stressors in each category.

International Stress Institute classification of stressors

General stressors	Physical stressors	Neuropsychiatric stressors	Psychosocial stressors	Occupational stressors
- fasting, starvation, malnutrition - overeating, force-feeding - physical trauma	- altitude, hypoxia, gangrene - burns - heat - electroshock - physical exercise - cold, frostbite - gravity, acceleration, deceleration - war, combat - hyperventilation, hyperoxia, compression - solar rays - toning rays - X rays - visible spectrum - magnetism, electromagnetic fields - immobilization, physical restraint - sound, noise - temperature in general - ultraviolet and infrared rays - ultrasound - vibration	- anxiety, restlessness - emotions - affliction, mourning - lack of affection, child care - examinations, tests - combativeness - handling (animals) - sensory deprivation - sleep deprivation - interviews - media - motivation - public speaking - stage fright	- captivity, imprisonment - catastrophes, cataclysms - weather, climate - overpopulation, crowding - culture - economic problems - family (divorce, delinquency, child abuse) - hospitalization, intensive care - aging - pollution - immigration, moving - social isolation - social problems - transportation, traveling - urban life, environment	- flying, aeronautics - architecture - air traffic control - armed forces - arts - athletics - criminality - dental arts - administrative work, office work - industry, commerce - law - medicine - driving - navy - nursing - parachuting - police - deep-sea diving - social work - education (teaching, studying) - retirement - unemployment

1. *General stressors*

The first category of stressors includes physical trauma; fasting or malnutrition or overeating. Like some physical stressors, these stressors trigger an alert reaction in the organism just by their specific effects. Even though the danger of overeating may not be perceived, obesity is bodily stress. In the food section, we will mention how eating habits and diets can traumatize the organism just as external agents do.

2. *Physical stressors*

The list of physical stressors is long and varied. Here are some examples. Overly intense physical exercise can trigger heart attacks in some predisposed people. People who have been shipwrecked emphasize the stress caused by cold on the high seas. In the San Francisco Chronicle, Nov. 1, 1977, it was pointed out that Mexican factory workers exposed to constant machinery noise when compared to a control group showed the following symptoms to a significant degree: nervousness, weight loss, heart attacks and decreased sexual desire. Tanner reported the same dangerous effects of noise on children living near a 12-lane highway in New York. These children had more difficulty than a control group in distinguishing similar sounds such as "gear" and "beer", "cope" and "coke" and thus had more difficulty in learning to read and write.

War is undoubtedly the most violent physical stressor with a multitude of stress agents: cold; heat; mud; mosquitoes; lack of independence, sleep and food; noise and confusion; distress; wounds; death, loss of combat comrades, etc. The stress is such that Janis cites a great number of cases of soldiers falling asleep on the firing line and fighters during the last war forgetting to take the most elementary precautions to ensure their survival, as though at such a level of stress the human being simply gives in to death.

3. *Neuropsychiatric stressors*

Neuropsychiatric stressors are related to environmental conditions or events which usually cause states of distress, anxiety, rage, sadness or fear or, if the trauma is intense, panic attacks, acute or chronic depression, obsessive thoughts, nightmares or hallucinations.

Laboratory experiments have shown many times that in a state of sensory deprivation, subjects manifest the following symptoms: disorientation, anxiety, depression and even hallucinations. Trappers in the far North and truckdrivers after long hours of monotonous driving report similar symptoms.

A bereavement or a serious accident generally causes the same effects: anxiety attacks, sleep problems, feelings of depression, lethargy, confusion, irritability, loss of emotional control, physical or mental. Total or partial amnesia of the traumatic event and nightmares complete the picture.

Tests, examinations and job interviews are familiar enough so we all have experienced the effect of neuropsychiatric stressors to varying degrees.

4. *Psychosocial stressors*

In his book, Future Shock, Alvin Toffler describes most of the psychosocial stressors of modern life. Although the good old days were no bed of roses, stress agents then were simple and, in general, foreseeable. Stress came mainly from physical threats or deprivation. Modern stress is more psychological; it is continuous, less controllable, more unexpected, aggravating and cumulative.

Adaptation demands come from all sectors of life: where to live, what to do, what lifestyle to adopt, what food to eat, how to dress, etc. Lifestyles today are as transitory as consumer goods. People relate to heroes and ideas which disappear rapidly, leaving them in search of a new identity. Lifestyles (homosexuality, vegetarianism, sports, etc.) are consumed the way life-sustaining products used to be consumed. An evening at the theatre becomes a happening, the choice of an automobile becomes a veritable creative project because of the variety of models and accessories available. There used to be one or two television stations; now there are cables, pay TV and programming on demand.

Technology accelerates the pace and rate of production. The pace of life is faster and faster. Objects, places and people are becoming transitory. Nowadays, it's easier to buy than to repair; we use paper towels and rent our cars. In 1966, 7,000 new products appeared on the American food market and in 1971, 42% were already things of the past. From 1950 to 1963, the number of soap brands went from 65 to 200. Toffler jokes that Shakespeare would be an illiterate today because he would understand only 250,000 of the 450,000 English words in common use.

Every day, new discoveries create new perspectives on life. It's said that in 50 years, man will live largely on marine resources (nutrition, recreation, habitation, etc.). We talk about the bionic man, birth technology... In 1938, airplanes reached a speed of 450 mph and in 1960, space capsules were traveling at 18,000 mph. Before 1500, 1,000 new books a year were published in Europe; in 1965, 1,000 new books appeared every day around the world. The information world bombards us every day with ideas and images that transform our view of reality. The average American is exposed to 560 commercials every day.

One American in four moves each year. In 1969, out of the 885,000 names in the Washington telephone directory, more than half were new listings. In large companies, management personnel have to move so often that "IBM" now stands for "I've been moved". M. Fried studied the reactions of people forced to move and found that many of them had reactions similar to people who had suffered a loss in the family. He concluded that these moves caused an intense stress reaction. Researchers have shown elsewhere that illnesses related to stress and mortality rates are higher among immigrants and people who leave farms to live in cities.

All these changes profoundly affect social and personal relationships. Moving means constantly having to form new relationships. Social mobility changes the human environment in which we evolve. Interpersonal relationships become functional. Social isolation increases, generating considerable stress.

Solitude causes a host of problems. No matter what the population group (age, sex, having or not having children), married people say they are less stressed and more satisfied than their unmarried peers, single, widowed or divorced. A study of 7,000 Californians over a period of 9 years showed that mortality risks are 2½ times as high among socially isolated single men than among men who are married or socially active and that this risk goes up to 4½ times among women between the ages of 30 and 49 who have few social relationships as compared with a group of women of the same age who have more frequent social interaction.

The nuclear family is also experiencing the same social upheaval. One person in four can expect to be divorced according to the latest statistics. And there is more heart disease, cancer and suicide among divorced people than married people. We also know that partners in an unhappy marriage suffer from more stress-related illnesses than happily remarried people.

As everyone knows, urban life does not solve isolation problems; it adds a range of major stressors. In 1850, there were four cities with a population of over one million; in 1960, there were 141. Overpopulation studies isolate stress factors such as economic problems, multiple daily contacts, noise, transportation, and the size and density of the population.

Population density is considered as a crucial factor. A study made in Manhattan, where the density is 100 people per 100 square metres, reports that 4 out of 5 persons suffer from psychiatric problems, one out of 4 from serious neurosis and there are twice as many suicides, twice as many accidental deaths and four times as many cases of alcoholism and delinquency. Other researchers confirm the problems related to overpopulation. Zimbardo parked his car on a Manhattan street and another in Palo Alto. In both cases, he chose a spot close to a university and opened the hood to indicate mechanical trouble. In New York, he observed acts of vandalism after seven minutes. Forty-six hours later, the car was a pile of scrap. In the same time lapse in Palo Alto, the car suffered no damage; a pedestrian even stopped to close the hood when it started to rain.

It is not easy to draw a direct link between population density and observed social problems, since these problems may be explained by other factors such as unemployment and poverty. To confirm the relationship, studies were made among animals and, although they do not permit definite conclusions, similar observations were reported. For example, the study of a deer population along the Maryland coast showed that when the population reached 400, 300 died in three weeks. Autopsies revealed adrenal hypertrophy and chronic kidney problems, two characteristic stress symptoms. Laboratory research has shown that when rats are crowded together, dominant males become aggressive and attack other males, babies and pregnant females.

So, although the city offers many physical stimulations, both cultural and social, some of these benefits are themselves stress agents or lead indirectly to stress factors: crowds, line-ups, lack of job security, family problems, noise, pollution, transportation problems, overpopulation and crowding.

Even though psychosocial stressors have always existed, research leads us to believe that today they are more numerous and intense than in the past. In fact, many authors agree that the human being has never before lived through such stress, thus making it necessary to prevent "future shock."

5. *Occupational stressors*

Work is a major source of positive stress but for many of us, it is a source of distress. Studies in organizations isolate stress factors in the job itself, the physical surroundings, the social environment and the role played. Unsatisfactory working conditions, too much monotony, ambiguous evaluations, overwork, employees' varying abilities to meet deadlines and to separate their professional lives from their personal lives are work-related stress factors. Inadequate lighting, non-functional desks, restricted space, and office layout contribute, among other things, to a stressful physical environment. Relationships between colleagues and the hierarchic structure can increase tension at work. Ambiguity, overwork or the nature of the role can cause problems.

All things being equal, it seems that stress increases in proportion to the responsibilities assumed. R. Jacob quotes a study according to which emotional stress linked to heavy responsibility precedes heart attacks in 91% of cases. On the other hand, stress can appear if there is too little responsibility. For example, blue-collar workers suffer more from boredom stress than do white-collar workers.

Some professions are more stressful than others: for example, air traffic control, medicine, intensive-care nursing and emergency-ward work. Sedentary workers have more heart attacks and die younger than people whose work requires physical effort.

On the other hand, work is an important factor in mental health. The unemployed are more likely to commit suicide, have ulcers and nervous depressions and to get divorced than people who work. As well, compared with housewives, working women are happier, communicate better with their spouses, say they are more satisfied with their marriages and in general feel better physically and mentally. But one person's happiness can cause unhappiness for another; compared with husbands whose wives stay home, men married to working women are less happy, less healthy, have more pressure at work and are less satisfied with their jobs and their marriages!

The list of stress agents shows how numerous and varied they are. Some of them occur every day. From dawn to dusk, we are assailed by a multitude of stress agents whether at work, behind the wheel or at home. It doesn't take much to reach the critical stress threshold.

4. Distress

When stressed, the human being is in a state of psychological alert, which activates a better perception of danger and motivates action, as emotions are an energy source for fight, flight or compromise solutions. Although stress can help the organism defend itself or fight to survive or live better by supplying the necessary physical or psychological energy, too high a level of activation can bring about a state of physical or psychological distress.

PHYSICAL DISORDERS

Nowadays, it is thought that stress plays an important role in triggering illnesses. By giving scores [1] to the changes which frequently occur in people's lives (See Table 2), Holmes and Rahe found a strong correlation between scores of 300 points on their scale (over a one-year period) and the incidence of some illnesses. Do the test yourself and you will see that this score is quickly reached.

---

1. These scores were set from a sampling of the American population and are comparable to scores from other samplings in other cultures.

TABLE 2

Holmes-Rahe Scale

Events	Points
Death of spouse	100
Divorce	73
Marital separation	65
Prison sentence	63
Death of close relative	63
Injury or illness	53
Marriage	50
Loss of job	47
Reconciliation with spouse	45
Retirement	45
Illness of family member	44
Pregnancy	40
Sexual difficulties	39
Increase in family	39
Change in financial situation	39
Death of close friend	37
Changing jobs	36
Change in frequency of domestic quarrels	35
Mortgage or heavy loan	30
Change in professional responsibilities	29
Child leaving home	29
Problems with in-laws	29
Great personal success	28
Wife returning to or leaving work	26
Beginning or ending studies	26
Change in habits	24
Problems with employer	23
Changing residence	20
Changing schools	20
Holidays	13
Minor infractions	11

To alleviate your fears, perhaps mistakenly, let's add that the Holmes-Rahe test can be easily criticized. The study does not account for individual differences in predisposition to illness (biochemical agents, psychological adaptive factors and available social support) nor for the fact that minimal and continuous stress can be as significant as major stress. In addition, the scale has less validity because it is self-evaluating, therefore subjective.

Although the results of the Holmes-Rahe test may be questionable, it is certain that stress is a source of abnormal manifestations or complication of pre-existing abnormalities which can lead as far as death. For some, stress may be the direct cause of many illnesses; for others, one of the causes of some illnesses along with physical factors. Rahe has even classified illnesses by the relative importance of physical and psychological factors. In illnesses such as migraines, back problems, stomach or duodenal ulcers or coronary ailments, psychological factors predominate while in botulism, for instance, physical factors are almost entirely dominant. Let's look at the conclusions of other researchers.

Selye cites the important role of stress in arterial tension, cardiac accidents, duodenal and gastric ulcers and many mental problems.

Friedman and Rosenman, reputable cardiologists, write: "Exercise, diet, family history and cholesterol level are important factors in cardiac illnesses, but the crucial factor in the accelerated increase of the rate of the illness is the ever-increasing rhythm of life."

McQuade and Aikman in a book on the physical effects of stress say it plays a role in heart attacks, hypertension, angina, arrhythmia, migraines, ulcers, colitis, constipation, diarrhea, diabetes, infections, allergies, cancer, backaches, headaches, arthritis and accident-proneness.

Schafer concludes his review of the literature by saying that stress increases the probability of the following illnesses : headaches, ulcers, insomnia, backache, high blood pressure, colds, arthritis, colitis, allergies, skin problems and addiction. In the last case, let's specify that Marlatt confirms the correlation between tension and the probability of alcoholism while still mentioning that drinking can temporarily reduce stress.

Despite differences of opinion, the researchers cited agree that stress plays an important, perhaps leading, role in three classes of illness : headache and backache, stomach and duodenal ulcers and high blood pressure.

PSYCHOLOGICAL DISORDERS

Stress causes not only physical illness but also symptoms of mental illness or mental illness itself. Some symptoms are benign and common such as fatigue, muscular tension, irritability or emotional withdrawal. Too much stress, however, can bring on depression and even schizophrenia.

The relationship between stress and mental illness remains nebulous. Epstein uses the notion of self-concept to describe the link between the two phenomena. According to him, although moderate stress helps enrich self-concept, heavy stress (such as a threat to physical integrity or self-esteem, loss of love objects, impotence in solving a problem and physical or mental over-stimulation) can rapidly unbalance self-concept functions. He defines these functions as follows : maintaining a favorable balance between pain and pleasure, assimilating new experiential data and maintaining self-esteem. If an imbalance occurs, the individual may become defensive in order to keep his self-concept intact, and varying degrees of pathological symptoms appear.

Many authors agree that defence mechanisms are ways of facing stress. They are thus considered as adaptation mechanisms rather than defence mechanisms. It can even be said that the neurotic personality is a general way of dealing with stress. The obsessive-compulsive subject, through a personality structure characterized by a rigidity of thought and a feeling of obligation without personal autonomy, avoids new experiences and thus overcomes the anxiety engendered by doubt and uncertainty.

Menninger has drawn up a five-level classification of defence mechanisms using an adaptation continuum. On the first level, he cites hyperactivity and over-intellectualizing and gives insanity as the most extreme defence mechanism. Laing and Bateson also see schizophrenia as the extreme solution to unbearable tension. These theories have been verified in specific population groups. Many researchers have shown that women suffering from breast cancer or parents of children with terminal illnesses use different mechanisms such as denial, rationalization, or isolation affect to react to stress and that their level of adaptation depends on the relevance and effectiveness of the mechanism in the situation. Denying the disease can prevent women with cancer from seeking the medical care needed, while denying the seriousness of the problem allows them to follow the treatment instead of committing suicide or panicking in the face of death. Other research on medical students shows that jokes and humour are used as mechanisms for dealing with examinations while professional language and certain technical manœuvers such as covering the face of a cadaver during an autopsy are cited as strategies for reducing stress.

States of profound distress can be provoked by micro-stressors as well as by macro-stressors. Depression, for example, is more likely to be caused by accumulated micro-stressors than by the precipitating event usually thought to be the source of the condition. Micro-stressors may vary: daily critici m, unrealistic goals, negative self-assessments, lack of social communication or an absence of positive rewards.

A bereavement, a serious accident or a particularly stressful experience such as a shipwreck are the best illustrations of macro-stressors. Reactions to them are so intense that they can easily cause a temporary or chronic traumatic neurosis. Lindemann describes the reactions to separation or bereavement as follows. At the somatic level, distress manifests itself as tightness in the throat, breathing difficulties, frequent sighing, a feeling of emptiness in the stomach and muscular fatigue. On the psychological level, subjects report feelings of unreality, emotional distance from others, intense preoccupation with the missing person, a tendency to be irritable and sometimes guilt feelings. On the motor level, agitation, difficulties in carrying out an organized activity and frequent lethargy have been observed. Some people react with hyperactivity to forget the loss; others develop psychosomatic illnesses such as ulcerous colitis and asthma or psychological problems such as agitated depression or interpersonal conflicts.

These symptoms disappear with time in most cases but, for some people, the adaptive neurotic state becomes chronic. They do not regain interest in daily activities, develop problems at work, show a great deal of dependence and live in an increasing state of generalized fear that many people attribute to a loss of self-confidence in one's ability to face stress.

The effect of an intense stress crisis often differs according to whether the individual faces it alone or with a large number of people. A collective disaster, a war or an earthquake often have positive consequences such as a clear decrease in delinquency rates or rates of admission to psychiatric clinics and a lower number of suicides. In the United States, researchers studied 140 cases of natural catastrophes. They observed that in spite of appalling circumstances, most individuals performed emergency tasks with common sense and humanity. Studying the reactions of the population after a tornado, Fritz observed the same behavior: in the half-hour following the tornado, 32% of people looked for missing persons, 11% helped victims and 35% devoted themselves to other urgent activities.

To conclude, the first reactions of emotional distress are adaptive and aimed at assimilating the stressful experience and regaining physical and mental strength. Problems often appear because this first step is evaded. Watzalwick, Weakland and Fisch point out that a problem is a normal difficulty of life that has been badly resolved. When a person feels attacked or destroyed by a stressor, any reaction of defence, depression, hyperactivity or intellectualizing helps to reestablish a balance and gradually regain energy. Selye himself notes that stress can, paradoxically, bring about beneficial changes insofar as the person is capable of dealing with it.

II
MANAGING STRESS

5. The problem-solving process

Philosophers and revolutionaries have dreamed of a stress-free life, a paradise of harmony and relaxation. Some proposed a spiritual route, a detachment from worldly goods and meditation. Others opted for social and political conscience and exhorted their followers to unite to create socioeconomic structures favoring individual respect and well-being. As valuable as they may be, these solutions are hardly realistic and offer no immediate remedies to the daily problem of stress.

In the first part of this guide, you were told about the nature of stress, the principal stress agents and the harmful effects of distress. In the second part, we will use this information to suggest an approach to self-managing stress that is within your reach, that you can begin on right away and which will help you make the life changes that are necessary. However, don't think that these are miracle recipes! A self-management approach requires patience and effort and a certain amount of skill and knowledge.

Self-management comes from a belief in internal rather than external control of one's direction in life. Many people believe that their lives are regulated by destiny; others, by events and they can only resign themselves to being powerless. For example, they do not feel responsible for their sickness or health. Others, conversely, believe in internal control. They show initiative, responsibility and independence. These people feel they have power over their behavior and their lives. Self-management is based on assuming responsibility for your life and believing that you have the power to maintain or modify your behavior according to your goals.

Some people think that self-management requires a great deal of "willpower." Recent analyses of human behavior show that, first of all, it requires mastering certain skills, mainly skill at solving problems, which is fortunate because present scientific knowledge has no explanation for the mysterious mental power called will-power. Exercising willpower is no different from self-management. Self-managing your life is exercising willpower.

When we speak of skill at solving problems, we are referring to being able to make a logical and structured approach to solving the problem. Such an approach (see Figure 6) requires a clear definition of the problem, listing and analyzing possible solutions, choosing a solution or solutions, applying the decision and, finally, evaluating the results obtained.

The problem-solving process can be represented as a circular process since the last stage, evaluating results, often shows that the problem is not entirely solved and a new problem-solving process is needed. Rarely can one solve a problem of any complexity in one try. Using stress to your advantage rather than to your detriment will undoubtedly require several problem-solving pro-cesses.

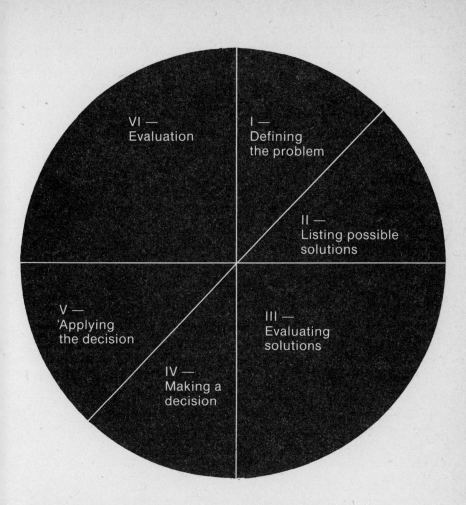

Figure 6: Illustration of problem-solving process

In these pages, we will guide you through the six phases of solving stress problems in your life. To define these problems, we will suggest a number of exercises which will help you see how your present behavior and your life environment contribute to the problems you have. We will then propose a set of major solutions or strategies for solving the problems. You will first have to analyze the relevance and effectiveness of these solutions and then make a choice of one or another solution. As it is rarely easy to act on these, we will give you information about behavior modification which will help you carry out your decision.

At the proper time, you will evaluate the changes achieved and you may realize that other changes are necessary. But since you will have mastered the problem-solving technique, you will then be able to self-manage these difficulties.

6. Defining the problem

What are your stress-related problems? We will now try to answer this question. To do so, we will first see how to define a problem in general and, second, apply this procedure to the stress problem.

HOW TO DEFINE A PROBLEM

Imagine that a friend of yours confides that he is stressed and depressed because his studies are not going well, and he asks you to help solve this problem. How would you answer or proceed? Before continuing to read this book, take a few minutes to think. You will undoubtedly note that if you truly want to help him, you will need more information on his situation. What questions would you then ask him? What information do you need to define the problem? Think again for a few minutes. Do you realize that a general method is necessary to define a problem or to gather information for solving it?

But let's continue our story and imagine that your friend says he has got only 70% in an examination when he was aiming at 80%. Unless you find his difficulty laughable, you will notice from this that a problem is a subjectively felt difference between a real situation and the ideal situation. Some students are satisfied with a grade of 70% but your friend is depressed by this result. It is not the real situation which is the problem but the variance between the fact (70% grade) and the ideal situation (80% grade).

To define a problem, the real situation and the ideal situation must both be known. The real situation and the ideal situation are defined by observable and measurable facts and behavior. Whether the problem is recent or has lasted for years, the behavior (actual and ideal) and the situation (actual and ideal) contain all the necessary elements for understanding its source or its continuance. Thus, to define the problem of stress in your life, instead of categorizing or labeling yourself as stressed, you must systematically analyze your situation and your behavior and see the variance between the reality and the desired situation. You will notice that the analysis bears on the difference between two situations or two behaviors and not on the "why" of the situation or behavior. In the area of stress, we do not seek to know why you suffer distress but how to minimize the gap between the real situation and the ideal situation.

HOW TO DEFINE STRESS PROBLEMS IN YOUR LIFE

In the first part of the book, we saw that stress is a state of the body when it perceives that its well-being is threatened and it must use its energies for self-protection. We also saw that when a stressor acts on a person, the impact depends on numerous variables, among them the nature and intensity of the stress agent and the characteristics of the person exposed to it.

To define the problems of stress in your life, you must first know the quality and quantity of the stressors to which you are exposed and, then, the state of resistance of your body to these pressures — in other words, your physical, psychological and social condition.

TO WHAT STRESSORS ARE YOU EXPOSED?

We have talked a lot about the principal stressors to which the human being is exposed. We will now suggest two exercises allowing you to identify the source and the nature of the stressors you face as well as the way these different stressors affect you.

Exercise 1

Using the list from the International Stress Institute (see page 37), make a list of the stressors to which you are exposed. To do this, mentally review several typical days from getting up to going to bed and write down all the stressors that occur.

Exercise 2

Now answer the following questionnaire to identify the type of stress that affects you most.

STRESS-TYPE EVALUATION QUESTIONNAIRE[1]

Circle the score which corresponds to your response. If the question is not relevant, score 0.

	Score
A) PERFORMANCE STRESS	
1. When I practise a competitive sport,	
— all my game suffers from a lack of concentration	3
— there are times in the game where my attention is not solely directed at game strategies	2
— my attention is concentrated on the game and I play my best	0
2. During a conversation with one or several people,	
— I often wonder about the best thing to say	3
— I don't like to give my opinion for fear that the others don't share it	2
— I have no difficulties	0
3. When I make love with a partner,	
— I have very little idea of what to do to satisfy myself or him/her	3
— we reach mutual satisfaction but irregularly	2
— we are usually confident that it will be pleasurable	0

---

1. Questionnaire adapted from Sharpe and Lewis (1977).

	Score

4. When I do demanding intellectual work,

— I frequently lose concentration and can't apply myself to the task **3**

— I work only in short periods broken up by long fruitless periods **2**

— I like the challenge and rapidly get down to the task **0**

5. When I have to make decisions which will affect the future of those close to me,

— I am desperately worried and I become very anxious without coming to a firm decision **3**

— I generally make a decision but not without a great deal of tension **2**

— I make a decision rapidly and keep to it **0**

6. When I am in a situation that could lead to sexual contact,

— I feel so anxious that I rapidly change the subject **3**

— I have difficulty expressing my real feelings **2**

— I have no difficulties **0**

7. When I have to act in public,

— I become panicky and find any excuse to avoid the situation **3**

— I have great difficulty controlling my tension **2**

— I am not unduly concerned by the presence of spectators **0**

TOTAL ....

	Score

B) FEAR STRESS

1. I practise a sport which involves a risk of physical injury,

— frequently	3
— from time to time	2
— never	0

2. I worry about getting sick,

— frequently	3
— sometimes	2
— never	0

3. When I am in situations which could lead to sexual contact, I am,

— very anxious	3
— uncomfortable and embarrassed	2
— relaxed	0

4. Facing certain objects or facts of life that most people accept without anxiety, I am,

— very tense and anxious	3
— nervous and uncomfortable	2
— as relaxed as they are	0

5. The probability of international war,

— puts me in a constant state of tension	3
— often makes me worried	2
— never bothers me	0

	Score

6. When I want to assert my rights and privileges,

   — I am afraid of being attacked   3

   — I'm afraid of infringing on someone else's rights   2

   — I don't hesitate to do so   0

7. When I have to travel far from home,

   — I feel very anxious and panicky and only want to go home   3

   — I look forward to the trip with worry and discomfort   2

   — I am totally at ease   0

        TOTAL ....

C) BOREDOM STRESS

1. When I get up in the morning,

   — I fear the boredom of the day ahead   3

   — I am not particularly stimulated by thinking of the day ahead   2

   — I am often stimulated by the day ahead   0

2. I find my work (or my studies),

   — routine, boring and unchallenging   3

   — generally interesting but with routine periods   2

   — very often stimulating and not excessively routine   0

	Score

3. When interacting with my partner,

- I find we have nothing in common to talk about or to do 3
- I have some interesting times separated by long periods of boredom 2
- I find these times generally stimulating and pleasant and the feeling is mutual 0

4. During sexual relations,

- there is little variety or new stimulation 3
- it is sometimes pleasurable 2
- I often have a pleasurable experience 0

5. I spend most of my leisure time,

- alone at home 3
- with the few friends I have 2
- in varied social situations 0

6. The intellectual tasks I have as a student or worker,

- drain my mind for any other stimulation 3
- stimulate me mentally a little but never enough 2
- stimulate me and give me a pleasing challenge 0

7. In social conversations,

- I am quickly bored by what I consider to be trite conversations 3
- I am sometimes interested 2
- I am usually interested 0

TOTAL ....

Score

D) FRUSTRATION STRESS

1. When interacting with my usual partner or my family, I find myself in the wrong,

	Score
— almost always	3
— often enough	2
— very rarely	0

2. My sexual needs are

	Score
— rarely satisfied	3
— irregularly satisfied	2
— satisfied	0

4. When I read or hear the news,

	Score
— I frequently feel powerless and manipulated	3
— I occasionally feel disturbed	2
— I don't feel involved	0

5. When I have to make important life decisions, I have the impression that I'll be the loser no matter what I choose,

	Score
— frequently	3
— occasionally	2
— never	0

	Score

6. When I think of the important problems that I am facing,

— I see no way out without losing	3
— I feel there are probably solutions that are going to take a lot of effort	2
— I think they can be solved with time and planning	0

7. I feel I meet life's challenges effectively,

— almost never	3
— occasionally	2
— usually	0

TOTAL	

E) GRIEF OR LOSS STRESS

1. I lost a relative or close friend

— very recently	3
— a few months ago	2
— a long time ago	0

2. Although it's been a long time since I lost someone or something dear to me,

— the pain I feel thinking about it is still strong	3
— I have moments, such as the anniversary of the loss, where I am still very affected	2
— I think of it now as an event in the past	0

3. Having recently left a job (or studies) which really interested me,

— I feel lost and can't get over it	3
— I have frequent memories of my previous happiness	2
— I have replaced this interest by another activity of equal value to me	0

Score

4. Having been recently separated or having lost a meaningful relationship,

— I feel very affected and it seems an irreparable loss 3

— it's taking considerable effort to move toward other relationships 2

— although I'm sad about this loss, I can move into other relationships 0

5. Now that I'm getting older,

— I panic when I think of my lost youth and the incapacities that old age will bring 3

— there are times when I feel I can no longer do the things I used to 2

— I feel myself heading toward a more peaceful existence 0

6. Having been deeply humiliated in the past,

— my self-confidence is weakened and I avoid conflict 3

— occasionally I think of what happened and feel a lack of confidence 2

— I have successfully isolated the event and my confidence has returned 0

7. Because I lost my health and was forced to change my lifestyle,

— I am constantly morose and depressed 3

— I try to accept the situation but few things have any meaning for me 2

— I am fighting hard but I'm succeeding at adapting 0

TOTAL ....

Write down here all the totals for each type of stress. You will use the results later on.
— Performance stress :
— Fear stress :
— Boredom stress :
— Frustration stress :
— Grief or loss stress :
You have just identified the stressors to which you are exposed and the type of stress to which you are most exposed. Now, let's see how much these stressors affect you.

WHAT IS YOUR THRESHOLD
OF RESISTANCE TO STRESS ?

The impact of a stressor depends in large part on the characteristics of the person exposed to it. Before predicting which stimuli will be stressing for someone, the physical and psychological conditions, the social situation and the previous history must be known.

Health, physical constitution, physical condition and the degree of relaxation are variables that at the physical level give rise to an advantageous or damaging stress reaction. Bad eating habits, lack of exercise and unhealthy living habits (lack of sleep, alcohol, tobacco, medications, etc.) increase our vulnerability to stress over the long term.

Psychological factors are also decisive in resistance to stress. These factors are many. Some are common to a population. For example, although pain is a universal phenomenon, Jews and Italians tend to exaggerate the sensations felt while Americans and Irish have a more phlegmatic attitude and "suffer" less.

Other factors, however, are peculiar to individuals. Friedman and Rosenman studied the type of personality susceptible to heart problems and singled out two types, A and B. According to these authors :

In the absence of behavior characteristic of type A, cardiac problems never arise before the age of 70 years, independent of the level of fat in the diet, cigarette consumption and lack of exercise...a healthy personality and certain modes of behavior are essential to a healthy heart...The characteristics of Type A are almost always behavior which triggers the flight-or-fight reaction. Consequently, type A is constantly in a state where the sympathetic system produces an excessive level of catecholamines (chemical products triggered by a stress state) resulting 1) in an increased level of blood cholesterol, 2) a decreased capacity to purify the blood of this cholesterol, 3) a prediabetic state and 4) an increased tendency for blood platelets and fibrinogens to deteriorate and agglomerate in the walls of veins and arteries. As the veins and arteries become obstructed, the heart must work harder and harder to circulate the blood through the body. Eventually, the arteries are so obstructed that the heart gives up.

The caricature of the type A is the overworked and hurried man who, simultaneously, eats breakfast, shaves, reads the newspaper and makes a phone call while listening to the latest stock-market news on the radio. The characteristics of this personality type are hyperactivity, drive, ambition, need to excel, competitive spirit, a state of constant alert, impatience, fighting against time, high demands for himself and for others, a need to dominate and self-assertiveness. Rosenman adds that subconsciously the person is vulnerable, tense, anxious, doubts the usefulness of a job or a career, fears failure and has difficulty adapting to sudden change.

An easy-going company president who uses type A personalities as vice-presidents is a good illustration of the type B personality. The characteristics of this type are openmindedness, a relaxed pace, attention to social and personal relationships and a reflective turn of mind.

Well before Friedman and Roseman's studies, Dunbar found common family-history characteristics in patients suffering from cardiac problems. For example, the men and women identified with their fathers as children and young adults, while feeling a great deal of hostility toward them. They particularly loved their mothers, yet easily dominated them. According to Dunbar, they concentrated on work because of this competition with their fathers whom they spent their lives trying to surpass.

Other research also shows a relationship between stress and personality traits. Researchers studying hospitalized burn patients found that the ones who recovered most quickly shared the following characteristics : independence, aggressiveness and a great deal of energy.

Without being as specific as the authors cited above, many thinkers believe that certain attitudes increase resistance to stressors. Selye favors altruistic egotism: succeed by being necessary to other people and thereby gaining their sympathy. Tache recommends taking up only real challenges. Holmes advises not taking the inevitable complications of life too seriously, having self-confidence and adopting an optimistic attitude. Culligan suggests hoping for the best, planning for the worst and taking whatever happens with a sense of humour. Boucher says that after trying everything, you only have to practise the seven gifts of a healthy mind and the three graces of an open heart. (See table 3).

TABLE 3

THE 7 GIFTS OF A HEALTHY MIND

Serenity: stay calm and let your mind wander when over-educated people are arguing.

Humour: only assume serious duties and constantly expect the worst.

Authenticity: constantly show one's weaknesses to emphasize the overwhelming qualities of others.

Wisdom: know that nothing is sure and everything will usually be done backwards.

Lucidity: know your own limits so well that those of your colleagues sometimes appear unbelievable.

Clairvoyance: foresee everyone's future while continuing to live day by day.

Integrity: make respect for your neighbor the most important thing after self-satisfaction.

AND THE 3 GRACES OF AN OPEN HEART

Tenderness: worry about your strength of character while cultivating your libidinous drives.

Spontaneity: preach the false to know the true while camouflaging your embarrassment as well as your surprise.

Pleasure: feel sorry for yourself while winning the lottery.

The stress reaction is largely determined by past experience. Some people are predisposed to stress: getting angry at the least pretext as they remember their fathers doing, or developing high blood pressure each time they stifle their anger as their mothers did.

Failure in a task increases subsequent performance stress in accomplishing the task. Knowledge of a task or a situation diminishes its stressful character.

A person's reactions to a stress agent depends on his internal environment: physical condition, psychological and social characteristics and previous history. They depend as well on the external environment in the largest sense of the word. Before predicting what conditions will be stressful for an individual, one must know not only the internal but the external environment: climate, habitat, economic situation, social milieu and personal relationships. Thus, a bereavement may be experienced very differently depending on the presence or absence of friends, the financial situation or the cultural meaning of such an event. The same applies to failure in school: the student concerned will feel more or less stress depending on past experience, attitudes, financial situation, the social support available or the expectations of the social environment.

When a stressor acts on a person, the impact depends on numerous physical, psychological and social variables. It would be unrealistic to try to control some of these factors but others easily lend themselves to a self-management approach. We will look at several strategies for this further on. For the moment, we suggest two exercises for assessing your physical condition and your personality type and for better defining your threshold of resistance to stress.

Exercise 3

Answer the following questionnaire to see if you are physically fit enough to deal with stress. Circle the score that corresponds to your answer.

PHYSICAL-CONDITION EVALUATION QUESTIONNAIRE	Score
1. Have you taken medication recently?	
— no	1
— yes	0
2. Have you been sick in the last month (other than a cold)?	
— no	1
— yes	0
3. Have you had an accident (even a minor one such as a cut) in the last month?	
— no	1
— yes	0
4. My usual sleep is	
— quite regular and restful	2
— occasionally disturbed	1
— very poor and irregular	0
5. How tired did you feel yesterday evening	
— pleasantly	2
— a little overtired	1
— exhausted	0

	Score

6. **If you practise yoga or if you take the time each evening for a hobby or other form of relaxation, give yourself a point** .... | 1

7. **Using the chart on page 145, find your ideal weight. If you are not more than 6 kilos over your ideal weight, score two points** .... | 2

   If your weight is between 6 and 12 kilos above the ideal, give yourself one point ... | 1

8. **Do you consume a lot of sugar (desserts, soft drinks, sugar in coffee or tea)?**
   — no .... | 2
   — yes .... | 0

9. **Are your eating habits regular and well-balanced?**
   — yes .... | 2
   — no .... | 0

10. **If you do not normally have more than 2 beers or one drink of liquor a day, give yourself one point** .... | 1

11. **How much intense physical exercise do you usually have each week?**
   — 1 hour or more .... | 2
   — ½ hour .... | 1
   — none .... | 0

12. **If you practise a sport, give yourself à point** | 1

13. **If you are not regularly seated while working, give yourself a point** .... | 1

14. **If you have made love in the last week, give yourself a point** .... | 1

	Score

15. How many cigarettes do you smoke on the average each day?

— 0	2
— 10 or less	1
— 11 or more	0

16. If you have not smoked a cigarette for five years or more, give yourself a point. If you do not smoke a pipe, give yourself a point. If you do not smoke cigars, give yourself a point .... | 1

Add up your total and multiply by four to obtain your score .... _____

_____ **0 to 25:** major changes are in order!

_____ **26 to 50:** you can do better!

_____ **51 to 75:** you can feel pretty satisfied about your lifestyle!

_____ **76 to 100:** everything's great!

Exercise 4

Friedman and Rosenman have drafted a short questionnaire to measure the type of personality susceptible to distress reactions. On a scale of 10 points, 0 as the minimum, characterize your reactions using the following questions. Do the test by yourself and get a friend to verify your evaluation.

PERSONALITY-TYPE
EVALUATION QUESTIONNAIRE

Questions	Points (0 to 10)
1. Are you competitive?	_____
2. Do you have an energetic personality?	_____
3. Do you make an effort to get a promotion at work or to succeed in the sports you practise?	_____
4. Do you like to do things quickly?	_____
5. Do you strongly desire public recognition?	_____
6. Do things and people easily make you angry?	_____
7. Do you often race against the clock? Are you conscious of time, work schedules?	_____
8. Do you strongly want to get ahead socially?	_____
9. Do you have several different activities?	_____
10. Do you become impatient when you are late or delayed?	_____
TOTAL	_____

If your score is 50 or more, you probably have a type A personality and your chances of a heart attack are approximately three times higher than type B people whose score is less than 50.

Now that you know how to define a problem, you are ready to specify your own stress problems. Using the results of exercises 1, 2, 3 and 4, analyze the present situation:

- What are the principal stressors presently in your life?
- From what type of stress do you suffer most?
- Does your physical condition permit you to increase your resistance to stress?
- Do you have a type A personality?

Add any other relevant information you have gathered so far from this book to these results.

Now, ask yourself about the ideal situation: describe your behavior, your physical and psychological situation and your environment. The gap between the actual situation and the ideal situation reveals the stress problems in your life. Don't end this first step in the problem-solving process without clearly specifying them! You've done it? Now go on to the second phase of the problem solving process: listing solutions.

7. Solutions: managing external stress agents

In chapter 6, you defined the stress problems in your life. Now you are ready to go on to the second phase of the problem-solving process: listing possible solutions. To reduce the gap between what you are living and the ideal situation, these solutions must act on the number and intensity of the stressors to which you are exposed or on your resistance to stress agents. Table 4 shows an overall view of strategies for these two objectives of stress management: managing external stressors and managing internal factors of resistance to stress.

Managing external stressors is organizing your life, as much as possible, to find the number and quality of stressors likely to produce an ideal environment. Many strategies are possible: time management, avoiding too many changes at once, anticipating stress, looking for meaningful activities, retreating from stressful situations, changing the stress agent or, in the last resort, living with the stress.

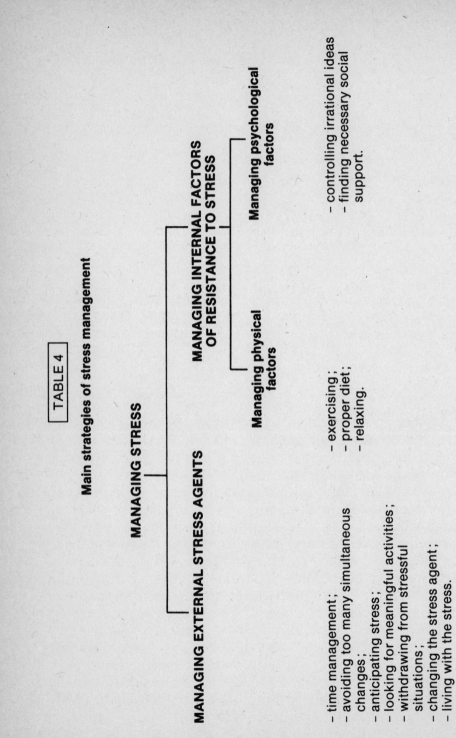

TABLE 4

Main strategies of stress management

MANAGING STRESS

MANAGING EXTERNAL STRESS AGENTS

MANAGING INTERNAL FACTORS
OF RESISTANCE TO STRESS

Managing physical
factors

Managing psychological
factors

- time management;
- avoiding too many simultaneous changes;
- anticipating stress;
- looking for meaningful activities;
- withdrawing from stressful situations;
- changing the stress agent;
- living with the stress.

- exercising;
- proper diet;
- relaxing.

- controlling irrational ideas
- finding necessary social support.

TIME MANAGEMENT

Some people are constantly stressed because they are overworked, cannot meet their deadlines, are forever putting off urgent tasks or using most of their time doing something other than what they really want to do. Added to the normal stress of life are a host of difficult situations and feelings of frustration and powerlessness.

Time management can be an apt solution to these difficulties. Managing your time is planning the time available to meet your goals in life. While this project may appear ambitious, it is realizable under two conditions: know your priority goals and have the means to attain them.

You can learn to manage your time. If this is the solution you need, you will find all the necessary information in chapter 11.

AVOID TOO MANY MAJOR CHANGES AT ONCE

Some changes require so much adaptive energy that it is dangerous to make them at the same time. The Holmes-Rahe scale can serve as a point of reference. For example, it's better not to change jobs when you are moving because these two life events cause considerable stress. If you are planning changes in your life, you will have to think about making them at different times to avoid reaching a stress level that can make you ill.

It's not always easy to plan all of life's changes. Some events occur no matter what provisions we have made. When these events occur, it is always good to plan a few days of rest and recuperation or a vacation afterwards to recoup the energy used.

ANTICIPATING STRESS

Anticipating a stressful event diminishes its impact. In their research, Glass and Singer showed, for example, that subjects' ability to predict the beginning and end of a loud noise considerably reduced the stress felt. In studying the effects of preparatory information on patients hospitalized for surgery, Janis also established the importance of anticipation. She found that overly optimistic patients found it more difficult to adapt to their condition after an operation than those who felt somewhat afraid before the operation and got information from nurses and doctors to reassure themselves. The first group experienced more vulnerability, powerlessness, disappointment and anger than the second. The absence of anticipatory fear before a potentially stressful event seems to inhibit the process of preparation or learning useful to adaptation. If you foresee entering a hospital or simply changing your eating habits, be informed in advanced about the consequences or effects of such an event.

As well as knowing how to recognize and use them, anticipated fears are assets in guarding against danger. Most of the time we tend to deny or minimize our fears when faced with stressful events. We can be severely self-critical about feeling fear as if it were a sign of immaturity. Fear is a normal emotion. As an indication of danger, it allows us to foresee the impact of stressors and thus diminish the potential stress of future events.

LOOKING FOR MEANINGFUL ACTIVITIES

As already mentioned, monotony can create as much stress as excessive stimulation. Looking for and practising meaningful activities thus becomes important in keeping an optimal energy level, avoiding boredom stress and providing constant vitality because you are working in your own interest. Selye has pointed out that to obtain peace of mind and self-realization most people need to work for a cause they consider useful.

An activity is meaningful when it furthers a goal, an interest or a preference. Whether at work, leisure or in your social or personal life, you must choose activities that give pleasure, a feeling of self-expression and self-realization and an impression of success in life however you define it.

Chapter 11 on time management can help you to identify and implement your priorities.

WITHDRAWING FROM STRESSFUL SITUATIONS

Withdrawing from a stressful situation can be an excellent strategy when the stress felt is greater than the optimal level. Several types of withdrawal are possible and the choice depends on the situation. You can withdraw temporarily by taking a rest break or by daydreaming for a short while. Sometimes a few minutes are all it takes to restore physical and mental energy. Vacations are sometimes needed to accomplish this. And, in some situations, a definite withdrawal such as ending a relationship, changing a job or giving up an activity is the only appropriate remedy for unbearable stress.

The withdrawal strategy should be used prudently so you do not risk fleeing situations which require presence and concentration. It is sometimes more useful to choose other solutions, especially in the case of a permanent withdrawal.

The relaxation breaks described in chapter 14 will be of benefit. They are excellent tools for temporarily retreating from stressful situations.

CHANGING THE STRESS AGENT

Some stress is caused by a well-defined agent: an air conditioner, traffic or smoke, for example. We tolerate a lot of useless stress when we could easily rid ourself of the stress agent. An air conditioner can be easily bought or repaired, a radio turned off, a window opened to air out a room. Often, we only have to think about our possibilities of action to act, especially if the stages of the project match our pace.

In some cases, however, changing the stress agent is hardly realistic: how do we stop traffic or change the university teaching system? Many people will say that only through political or social action can we, in the long term, modify a society's living conditions and, like Toffler, they advocate social changes to reduce the stress of modern life.

LIVING WITH STRESS

Living with stress is an adaptive solution when it is difficult or impossible to bring about a change by resorting to other solutions or when a subsequent benefit causes the actual stress. The mother of a family will put up with long sleepless hours to care for a sick child; a student will accept the stress of examinations to obtain a degree.

However, this situation holds several risks: one can easily live with stress by habit because of a defeatist attitude or victim behavior. In this case, this solution increases stress. Self-examination of the appropriateness of this choice is always profitable.

As you can see, many types of behavior are possible in managing external stress agents. As soon as you realize that the number and intensity of the stress agents to which you are exposed exceed or will exceed the acceptable threshold, you can resort to the most appropriate type for you.

8. Solutions: managing internal factors of resistance to stress

Stress management does not only consist of managing external stress agents but also of managing internal factors of resistance to stress. Managing internal factors of resistance to stress permits increasing the body's sensitivity threshold to stressors or improving its capacity of adapting to stress. Selye believed that adaptation energy is limited, that it drains away, causing senility and death. Although this theory has not been confirmed, we all know that being in good physical and mental condition helps us overcome daily difficulties and inevitable life crises. Mental and physical health acts as a filter to reduce or cancel out the impact of stress agents. Physical and psychic energy is precious, so why waste it? And why not try to save it so you have a more satisfying life?

Managing internal factors of resistance to stress means adopting living habits which minimize physical and psychic efforts while maximizing performance. Exercising, eating properly, relaxing, controlling irrational ideas, giving oneself the necessary social support and alternating tension and relaxation are all useful strategies for reaching this goal.

EXERCISE

The link between physical well-being and overall personal well-being has been recognized for a long time. Exercise is an important deciding factor in keeping physically fit; exercise acts directly on muscular strength, joint flexibility, heart efficiency, blood circulation in the lungs and all the vascular system. Exercise lets us digest better, look better and feel better. Unlike a machine, the more we use the body, the better shape it is in. It's not a matter of becoming an athlete but of keeping in shape to be more capable of responding to the many demands of daily life and have enough energy in reserve to face the unexpected. If necessary, refer to chapter 12 for further information on this strategy.

EATING PROPERLY

A good diet gives the body the right amount of the elements essential to its functioning and avoids products that are harmful to the health. Much research has shown that presently we are overfed and undernourished. How can the body resist stress agents if it lacks fuel or if unsuitable fuel is provided? Overeating and eating harmful foods stress the body because this impedes normal functioning and, at times, directly harms living cells.

Chapter 13 deals with nutrition; it will guide you in the choice and quantities of the foods you need.

RELAXING

Incessant activity and daily worries are constant sources of tension, so the organism needs periods of relaxation to regain its strength. One night's sleep is often not enough, especially when sleep is disturbed by physical or mental tension. People who suffer from intense stress and have a special need for all their adaptation strength are those who sleep the worst.

Nowadays to relax, we often resort to rapid but doubtful methods such as smoking a cigarette, gulping a tranquilizer, smoking marijuana or having a drink. Present statistics on the use of legal and illegal drugs are alarming, more so because we know the deleterious effects of these drugs on the body. While almost 50% of the population smokes cigarettes, we know that tobacco abuse increases lung cancer risks by 700%, quadruples the risk of cancer of the vocal cords as well as immeasurably increasing the probability of other diseases of the lungs, liver, blood circulation, heart and nervous system.

Because of the pleasant physical sensation they impart and the way they reduce anxiety or tension, drugs are an immediate solution to excessive stress, but almost all specialists point out the many problems they cause. Drugs can cause harmful side effects, physical or psychological dependence and a number of illnesses. Many specialists question even the use of legal drugs such as painkillers, sleeping pills and tranquilizers. Do you know that every year in the U.S., enough aspirins are sold to treat 17,000 million headaches a year, the equivalent of one pill every four days for each man, woman and child?

Many relaxation methods, more natural and safer than drugs, can be used to reduce the psychological effects of tension, thus slowing down adrenaline secretion and allowing the parasympathetic nervous system to fulfill one of its functions — relaxing the muscular system and soothing the body. Meditation, Jacobson's progressive relaxation, Therese Bertherat's warm-ups and certain relaxation breaks are some of the techniques for doing this. We will discuss them in chapter 14. The relaxed state you will reach by using one or another of them is a remarkable antidote to stress.

CONTROLLING IRRATIONAL IDEAS

A number of irrational ideas are a constant source of energy loss and stress. Irrational ideas are often the cause of intensely unpleasant emotions such as shame, remorse, guilt, rage or melancholy. And how much time is lost in mulling over impossibilities!

Irrational ideas are as numerous as they are diverse. They are about oneself, others or life in general. For example, you feel you must succeed at everything or that life should always be easy. Failure is terrible or a public-transport strike is a catastrophe. Living in North America with such ideas is an ominous thing.

Irrational ideas are the expression of introjected or projected standards or pseudo-truths. Let's take the idea of perfection. We live in a conformist society, where we learn or are taught to achieve goals according to a certain model. Conformity is useful in learning, but becomes a handicap for those who forget their personal style. So many people end up feeling inadequate when they should be questioning the notion that there is a perfect way of doing things. Being perfect is being as good as one can be in the time one is prepared to devote to an activity, not emulating a model.

To eliminate irrational ideas, we suggest adopting a rational emotional strategy that we will describe in chapter 15. Although it requires a certain discipline, this technique is simple to understand and use and can eradicate avoidable emotional problems.

GETTING THE NECESSARY SOCIAL SUPPORT

One of the problems most frequently named in literature on stress and contemporary society is that of social isolation. A study of 7,000 Californians over a 9-year period showed that, independently of health or income, mortality risks are higher among socially isolated men and women than among those with continued social and personal relationships. In this research study, social support came mainly from a spouse, the family, friends or various organizations. Even though the effect of social isolation varies from one person to another, the absence of meaningful human relationships causes a considerable number of more or less harmful effects: depression, anxiety, illness and even, we have seen, premature death.

Several theories have been formulated to explain the relationship between social isolation and stress. We know that interpersonal relationships satisfy certain fundamental human needs. In fact, through social or intimate contacts, we fulfill our needs for affection, acceptance, social inclusion, sensuality, public recognition, etc. Interpersonal relationships are also an important source of feedback and support. They allow responsibility-sharing, problem-solving and avoidance of useless errors; they give the necessary stimulation for achieving personal goals. Interpersonal relationships help us feel solidarity with others, giving us comfort, encouragement and ease.

Social isolation is, in itself, a source of stress and also increases the body's vulnerability to stress agents. Socially isolated people suffer from lack of affection. The resulting state of suffering or tension easily encourages them to adopt harmful strategies for reducing stress such as alcoholism, drugs or overeating.

As is easily understandable, there are no norms in the area of interpersonal relationships. Some people love solitude and benefit greatly from it. Others need close personal relationships and a network of social acquaintances. Others again have very few close friends and are satisfied with that situation. It is up to each individual to ensure that he or she has the social support needed.

ALTERNATE TENSION AND RELAXATION

Every performance requires physical or psychic tension. In running, for example, the hamstring pulls the lower leg backwards while the quadriceps pulls the leg forwards. In the first stage, the hamstring, relaxed at the outset, contracts to create the desired movement, then the quadriceps takes over to contract the knee muscles and bring the feet forward. Intellectual performance also requires tension. This manifests itself in febrility or anxiety. Performance anxiety, properly controlled, is not only inevitable but desirable. Emotions are an energy source. They activate the body's alertness center and increase the adrenaline level. Thus, they positively influence the physical strength available. As well, motivation to outdo yourself increases your endurance for a task.

Although every performance requires tension, we are often too tense and we forget to respect the basic law of effort, namely an alternation between tension and relaxation. Too much tension rapidly becomes a resisting force which slows down movement or performance. In running, for example, the hamstring is still partially contracted at the moment when the quadriceps begins to flex to bring the leg forward. This contraction requires an additional energy expenditure so that the antagonistic muscle, the quadriceps, can do its job. To maximize the available energy, the muscle used must be tensed and its antagonist optimally relaxed. Also, a relaxed muscle is longer than a flexed muscle; this elongation permits a stronger subsequent contraction and accelerates movement without additional effort. Similarly, intellectual tension and relaxation must alternate to avoid energy loss or rapid exhaustion. Forcing oneself to study for hours at a stretch only causes fatigue and distraction. In the same way, too much tension during an examination or a job interview considerably decreases performance.

The secret of optimal performance lies in a balance between tension and relaxation. All physical or mental activity can be conceived of in the Oriental fashion as a game of opposing forces and a constant balance sought between the yin and the yang, thought and action, effort and rest, concentration and relaxation. Ultimately, what is important is not so much the force one deploys in reaching a goal as the skill at relaxing the antagonistic force at the right time.

To save physical and mental energy, you must learn to use only the strength needed to accomplish a task. A high level of stimulation may be necessary for some activities, such as playing tennis or making love, but such a level is superfluous in other activities such as reading or playing the piano.

The reticular formation, seat of the body's alertness center, can be influenced voluntarily. For example, talking to yourself before a job or making sounds during the sexual act can increase activation, while practising the rational emotional strategy or relaxing lowers it. Thus the stimulation level can be adjusted advantageously depending on the activity underway, or the task can simply be postponed until the stimulated level is suitable. In fact, to avoid useless stress, it is better to delay a task rather than carry it out when over-stimulated or so under-stimulated that there is no motivation to succeed.

Alternating tension and relaxation may seem to be child's play since there are so many ways of doing it (daily sleep, vacations, relaxation breaks) but the pace of modern life is so frantic that a change of attitude is often needed in order to do so. Ecologists say that today we are using up energy as if the supply were inexhaustible. Many people behave this way with their health. Learn to pay attention to your level of tension, to use only the tension needed for a task and to alternate tension and relaxation.

The list of solutions proposed in this and the preceding section shows you the variety of strategies possible for solving stress problems. You can manage external stress agents to optimize their number and intensity and you can raise your threshold of resistance to stress by adopting a lifestyle that keeps you physically and psychologically fit. How do you choose among these solutions ? Follow the guide...

9. Choosing a solution

We have just reviewed several solutions to stress problems. Obviously, you will not be able to apply all these strategies : first, because they are not all equally relevant in your case and, second, because the effort required will be so great that you will quickly abandon the changes begun and return to your normal lifestyle. This section, on the third stage of the problem-solving situation, aims at helping you choose the most appropriate solution to the problems you have already identified.

Making a choice means evaluating the solutions according to relevant criteria, then adopting the solution which has received the highest mark. Obviously, an objective attitude is needed for a strict analysis. You must avoid any prejudices for or against the solutions being analyzed and try to see all the links between the problem, the solution and the context in which it will be applied.

Let's now look at the relevant analysis criteria for stress. The most important is undoubtedly matching the solution to the problem to be solved. The solution must aim at the most favorable stress level while respecting your personal comfort zone. What do we mean by these terms? We have seen that a favorable stress level is a source of efficiency, motivation, interest and competence and, to obtain this objective, there must be a personal balance between certain factors of life, weighed according to their intensity, such as self-interest and the interests of others, work and leisure, thought and action, risk and security, change and stability, stimulation and tranquility, personal needs and environmental demands.

As for "personal comfort zone," Schafer defines it as the rate and variation of stimulation which each person needs to feel comfortable and healthy. Each person has a personal comfort zone. One person will feel good with much intense stimulation, another will prefer a low or moderate level of stimulation, and a third will feel as comfortable at a fast pace as at a slow.

Although we expect that the "favorable stress level" and the "personal comfort zone" will coincide for an individual, this is not always so. A businessman who likes to work under constant pressure is often under excessive stress and it is very likely that he will have cardiac problems. On the other hand, some housewives feel uncomfortable returning to the job market, although they suffer boredom stress at home : their personal comfort zone is lower than the most favorable stress level.

Happily, the personal comfort zone is not fixed once and for all. Energy level and temperament are determining factors but education and environment are just as important. A comparison between the Occidental and Oriental paces of life shows the influence of culture on lifestyle.

You can therefore modify your personal comfort zone so that it will be comfortable as well as healthy. The favorable stress level varies from one person to another. Heed your needs.

The possible consequences of the solution make up the second analysis criterion. Consequences may be of several kinds : financial, familial, psychological, physical, social, etc. Taking a vacation may at first appear to be a good solution to work-related stress, but if you run the risk of losing your job by heading for the sun when your boss is counting on you to balance the budget, you will certainly weigh the pros and cons of this decision. The more you develop the habit of seeing the possible consequences of a solution, the more you increase your chances of making an enlightened and wise decision.

Some solutions, such as meditation,can be effective in the long term but may bring little change over a short period. Others, such as delegating a task, can immediately reduce stress. The nature of the problem indicates the relevant choice. Generally, it is better to adopt a short-term strategy if the problem is urgent and long-term strategies to avoid future stress.

The material implications of a solution must also be analyzed. How much time, money, human resources, etc. will the problem require? Being able to see all the concrete implications of a solution facilitates decision-making and, obviously, the application of the final decision.

To sum up, let's mention two other analysis criteria : simplicity and interest. Your stress problems will not be solved by choosing complex solutions or those that are not in keeping with your interests and aptitudes. These criteria are very subjective; take your personality into account if you want to identify simple, easy and interesting solutions.

Use the following table to mark the salient points of your analysis. First make a list of the solutions proposed and add the solutions you have found yourself. Mark each solution on a scale of 1 to 5. Use the "Other" column to include important analysis criteria that have not been mentioned here. On another sheet, write down the facts justifying your mark so you won't omit anything in the final analysis. You can add up the marks for a solution or weigh each mark in advance, using the priority analysis criteria appropriate to your case. The analysis lets you synthesize the data, thus facilitating your decision : don't neglect it.

TABLE 5

Solution analysis grid

Solutions	Matching the solution to the problem	Consequences	Character: Long-term or short-term solution	Material implications	Simplicity	Interest	Other
			Criteria				
1.							
2.							
3.							
4.							
5.							
6.							
7.							
8.							
9.							
10.							

Now that the advantages and disadvantages of each solution have been analyzed, a solution or group of solutions must be chosen. Compare the solutions, make a list and decide.

You may have difficulty putting equally valuable solutions in order. However, it's better to make the decision than to keep beating about the bush. With experience you will be able to verify the suitability of your decision, then make the necessary adjustments.

10. Applying the solution

So many people make decisions, then never go on to apply them! Often, the first three stages of the problem-solving process have been skipped; it's easy to understand why the decision goes unheeded. Sometimes, however, a poor application of the decision is at fault.

Planning how to apply a decision is the best way to ensure doing it. Planning a deed means foreseeing the place, time, deadlines, methods of evaluation and strategies of application. Planning a project increases motivation and facilitates carrying it out.

Among the strategies of applying a decision, we would like to mention behavior-modification strategies in particular. These strategies are highly useful in making a behavioral change, whether acquiring a desired behavior or getting rid of unwanted behavior.

When we do not succeed at carrying out a personal decision, we often tell ourselves, or are told, that we lack willpower. It's always been believed that willpower is a mysterious attribute over which we have no control. Some people have it, others don't. Today we know that certain kinds of behavior help us have willpower and, consequently, carry out a decision. For example, imagine that to increase your resistance to stress, you have decided to go on a diet. You come home in the evening and your friend has just made your favorite cake. He or she is in the middle of eating a large piece and, when you refuse a portion, you're told that diets are useless and frustrating. It will be a lot more difficult for you to have willpower in this situation than if your friend has bought fresh fruit for dessert, has excellent eating habits and compliments you on your new figure.

In this example, you will notice that the target behavior (keeping on a diet) will be much easier if preceded by appropriate stimuli (seeing fruit), is easy to achieve (presence of a role model) and is followed by positive reinforcement.

Behavioral modification can be grouped into three large categories. You can act on the reinforcing stimuli, act on behavior and act on previous stimuli. Let's explain these technical terms.

ACTING ON REINFORCING STIMULI

Some stimuli increase the probability of certain kinds of behavior. We call them reinforcements. A weekly pay cheque reinforces motivation to work, and weighing oneself daily reinforces the will to lose weight for a person on a diet. In the same way, thinking of a planned trip is a fantasy that reinforces the act of saving money or completing a difficult job. As the examples mentioned show, reinforcements can be very varied. They can satisfy our primary needs (thirst, hunger, sex) or our secondary needs (power, prestige, attention, etc.). Their source can be oneself or others. In the latter case, the reinforcement is more chancy, because we cannot control the people around us.

A number of behavioral modification strategies are based on reinforcement. In fact, given the effect of reinforcement on behavior, a change can be made much more easily by following desirable behavior with a reinforcement or by eradicating undesirable behavior by withdrawing the usual reinforcement.

Reinforcing or rewarding desired behavior is a simple and effective strategy. All that's needed is to apply the reinforcement as soon as possible after the desired behavior and only if the desired behavior occurs.

Some questions may help in finding reinforcements. Run through the following list of questions to find reinforcements that you can use at the opportune moment. When answering, account for the source of the reinforcement, whether it be yourself or others. It's better to have easily accessible reinforcements than to count on the goodwill of others.

TABLE 6

Useful questions for identifying reinforcements [1]

1. What things would you like to have?
2. What are your major interests?
3. What are your pastimes?
4. With whom do you like to be?
5. What do you like to do with these people?
6. What do you do for entertainment?
7. What do you do for relaxation?
8. When you feel like dropping all inhibitions, what do you do?
9. What do you do that makes you feel good?
10. What would you like to receive as a gift?
11. What things are important to you?
12. What would you do with $10, $50 and $100 that just came out of the blue?
13. What do you do with your pocket money each week?
14. What daily habits (even the most innocuous) do you have?
15. Do you adopt a certain behavior rather than the target behavior?
16. What would you hate to lose?
17. What daily activity could you give up most easily?
18. What are your favorite fantasies?
19. What scenes or images give you pleasure?
20. Can you visualize your condition when you reach your goal?

1. Questionnaire adapted from D.L. Watson and R.E. Tharp (1977).

The more closely a reinforcement follows behavior, the more it increases its probability. Although we learn with age to act for future gratification, immediate rewards usually have more influence over behavior than long-term rewards. It's difficult to keep to a diet because the act of eating brings a more reinforcing immediate gratification than the long-term prospect of a good figure. Thus the reinforcement must be applied as early as possible after the target behavior. One way of eliminating often inevitable delays is to choose easily accessible reinforcements or to give yourself points for the desired behavior and add them up to be entitled to a later reinforcement. For example, you give yourself 10 points for each hour of studying and 100 points gives you the right to an evening off.

It is essential to apply the reinforcement only if the desired behavior occurs. In fact, if you apply the reinforcement without having behaved as desired, you will increase the probability of unwanted behavior. For example, if you wish to learn to concentrate and if you decide that after an hour of concentration, you are entitled to a hot bath which you adore, taking the hot bath after an hour of daydreaming will reinforce the probability of daydreaming the next time you study. Be very careful to apply the reinforcement only if you have behaved as desired.

Unwanted behavior is often reinforced without our knowledge. For example, immediately after lighting up a cigarette, you think of the relaxation you get from tobacco. Just thinking this reinforces smoking behavior. Eliminating the usual reinforcement for unwanted behavior reduces its occurrence. You can also apply the usual reinforcement after desired behavior, namely thinking that you will relax each time you resist lighting a cigarette.

ACTING ON BEHAVIOR

Some goals require developing new behavior or new skills. Here are several useful strategies for doing this. The choice depends on the situation and the goal.

When the target behavior is in several stages, it can be divided into sub-goals and the successive stages of the behavior can be reinforced. We often lack "willpower" because the goals aimed at are complex and difficult to reach. The golden rule in behavioral modification is to proceed by simple, logical steps when there is an ascending order of difficulty. Thus if your objective is to make friends, you give yourself a reinforcement each time you speak for two minutes each to two people in your class or your office. Once this behavior is acquired, you reinforce a second intermediate behavior, such as talking for 10 minutes to the same people or talking for two minutes each to five people. As you can see, breaking down the target behavior into intermediate behavior varies according to your objective and your personality. As well, errors can easily arise in the analysis. If you do not succeed at establishing a behavior, it may be that it is too difficult: then find an intermediate behavior as the first stage.

An often effective strategy is adopting behavior incompatible with the unwanted behavior and following it with a positive reinforcement. For example, practising relaxation when you are worried and rewarding it by listening to your favorite record decreases the probability of worrying. It should be stressed here that relaxation can always be profitably used as behavior incompatible with avoidance behavior or phobic behavior.

Practising target behavior in reality or in your imagination, that is, outside the situation, increases the probability of the behavior occurring later in the situation where it should. For example, from now on you want to be able to refuse an overload of work to avoid a large source of stress in the office. When you are alone, you can see how to make it possible, what you will say, what you will do. In other words, make a mental movie of the target behavior down to the smallest detail and when possible, play your role out loud. If not, imagine the scene. Follow either exercise with a positive reinforcement to increase the probability of the behavior. To avoid the obvious danger of this strategy, put it into action as soon as possible , otherwise you will never be able to transfer what you have learned in the imaginary situation to the real situation.

Learning by imitation can also prove to be a very useful strategy in some cases. Giving yourself a good role model and taking the time to observe it often facilitates learning. For example, take a dancing course instead of staying alone in your bedroom and practising movements for which you only know the rudiments : your progress will astonish you !

ACTING ON ANTERIOR STIMULI

Anterior stimuli are any event or change in the environment before or at the time of the appearance of certain behavior and which influence this behavior. Seeing a cake can give you the urge to eat it, for example.

With time, some anterior stimuli acquire the power to trigger behavior. Having a coffee encourages smoking; sitting at a desk encourages concentration. These are called discriminatory stimuli. Some behavior is triggered by a single discriminatory stimulus; others, by several. People who overeat often react to several signals, such as seeing food, internal tension or boredom.

Acting on anterior stimuli consists of controlling the events prior to behavior. In the first stage, the stimuli must be identified. Then, as the case may be, they can be avoided, modified or gradually reduced. For example, to stop smoking, you can avoid having a coffee over a certain period or restrict yourself to smoking in only one room of the house. An alternative strategy is to set up stimuli that induce the desired behavior. Dressing as soon as you get up can become a stimulus for getting down to work. And don't forget that by applying a reinforcement after desired behavior, you will further increase its probability.

Stop reading now and see if certain behavioral modification strategies can help you apply the solutions you have chosen for solving your stress problems. First observe your behavior, the anterior stimuli and the subsequent stimuli and then choose the most appropriate strategies for your goals. In Table 7 you will find a list of different strategies.

Before putting them in action, plan all the other modalities of applying your decision: schedule, place, tools, calendar, control or evaluation method, etc. Are you ready? Get started.

Different behavioral modification strategies

I. Act on reinforcing stimuli:
- plan reinforcements;
- apply the reinforcement if you behave as desired;
- don't apply the reinforcement if you have not behaved as desired;
- remove the usual reinforcement of unwanted behavior and reinforce the desired behavior.

II. Act on behavior:
- reinforce the successive stages of the target behavior;
- use behavior incompatible with the unwanted behavior (and reinforce this behavior);
- practise the desired behavior, in reality or in imagination (and reinforce this practice);
- learn by imitation.

III. Act on anterior stimuli:
- in the case of unwanted behavior, avoid or modify the anterior stimuli of the behavior or reduce the incidence of the stimuli;
- in the case of desired behavior, choose and set up stimuli which can trigger the desired behavior.

III

FIVE IMPORTANT STRATEGIES

11. Time management

So many people feel they are not doing what they want in life! So much tension is caused by poor time management! You are undoubtedly familiar with the stress of an overloaded schedule or the frustration caused by daily restrictions keeping you from accomplishing your goals. How many students, for example, find themselves the day before an exam with a pile of disordered notes to study although, at the beginning of the term, they had resolved to study regularly.

Time management is a technique which helps you reach your objectives. Managing your time means planning the priorities of each day so that you receive daily confirmation that you are living your life as you want to. Managing your time is avoiding a host of stressful situations and extreme states of over-stimulation or under-stimulation; it is living at what you feel to be the most meaningful pace of life.

People often think time management requires excessive scheduling, counting every minute and racing against the clock. Unless these are your objectives, this is not necessary. Although it may seem self-contradictory, time management lets you enjoy more freedom. A daily agenda planned with your goals in mind lets you spend more time on your interests and desires and gives you the feeling of having the time to do what you want.

Many people find it difficult to manage their time because they have not properly identified their life priorities or simply do not know what they are. People who manage their time adequately know what they want to be or have. At some times, they may re-assess their situation and make changes, but these are mere episodes. Generally, they know where they're going.

Other people find it difficult to achieve their goals because they do not have the behavior needed for good time management. Managing time involves mastering a certain technique. By this we understand a range of behavior and attitudes which facilitate and favour achieving one's goals. We will talk about the following aspects: evaluating time use, applying management principles to time, dealing with procrastination and setting up favorable material and psychological conditions.

Do you want to learn time management?

The first step is to identify your life priorities. What short-term, medium-term and long-term objectives do you wish to attain? What are the projects dear to you? The following exercise from Lakein can help you. Take three sheets of paper and proceed as follows:

1. On the first sheet, write the answers to the following question as quickly as possible: What are your objectives in life? What would you like to achieve at the personal, family, social, professional and financial level? You have two minutes to answer. Complete this part before going on to the second step.

2. On the second sheet, also in two minutes, answer the second question: What are your objectives for the next three years? How do you want to spend the next three years of your life? Complete this part before going on to the third step.

3. On the third sheet, still in two minutes, answer this last questions: What are your objectives for the next six months? If you learned you were going to die in six months, what would you do from now until then?
4. Go back to each sheet and add all the details needed for understanding or improving each point.
5. You now have three lists of objectives. In comparing them, you can note resemblances, differences and contradictions that will help you draft a single list of priorities. To do this, Lakein suggests an ABC marking: A, for highly valued objectives; B, for average value and C, for those of least importance. Go back to the three lists of objectives and rank each activity using this scale. Remember you are the sole judge of the importance of each activity. Rank them as accurately as you can and after experimenting over a limited period of time revise your approach if you are not satisfied with the results. This revision can be done periodically, since priorities vary with time.

If you have not succeeded in completing Lakein's exercise, your lists probably contain objectives which are not truly priorities in your life at this time. They may be introjected or outdated objectives. Introjected objectives are those learned in childhood, inculcated by parents and society at an age when a personal identity has not yet been established. Often these objectives are not questioned in adulthood. Continuing to conform to the norms and standards of those who raised you when you want a different life inevitably leads to time management problems. Here is how to discover introjected objectives and gradually substitute self-determined objectives.

- in use, you will see that these objectives which have been evaluated as priorities do not take up a substantial amount of your time;
- you always put off attaining these objectives and feel somewhat guilty about it;
- you achieve these objectives as a "chore," a "duty," a "moral obligation" without feeling you have made a personal decision.

Although they may not belong in the introjected category, some objectives have been such a priority in our lives that we don't realize at times that they are outdated. For example, three years ago you spent 80% of your time studying. You continue to do so, out of habit, although you now have a greater need for personal relationships to satisfy your objectives. To discover outdated objectives, proceed as follows:

- go back to your list of objectives and ask yourself if these objectives are priorities today;
- carefully compare the answers to Lakein's third question with the answers given to the first two. If the objectives on the third list differ from those on the first two, the first two undoubtedly include outdated objectives.

Lakein's exercise has let you take stock of your short- and long-term priorities. Good time management consists of achieving those objectives. In principle, you are using your time optimally by carrying out type A activities and postponing or spending less time on type B and C activities.

In the second step, evaluate your use of time. This is an excellent way of diagnosing scheduling problems, then making the necessary corrections.

1. Using the weekly schedule that follows, make as many copies as necessary to write in all your activities, from getting up to going to bed, for two or three weeks. Be careful to choose typical days or weeks. Begin this exercise now and take care to fill in the schedule as you go, so you don't omit anything. Write in your main activities but don't forget coffee breaks, telephone conversations, etc.
2. Add up the hours spent on each activity in your week ; for example, 25 hours of study, 30 hours of classes, 6 hours at the movies, etc. Stay as close as possible to the original list of activities.
3. Now mark all the activities which further your type A objectives with an A and give a B or a C to those which further your type B or type C objectives. Many activities are part of daily routine : mark them R.
4. Add up the number of hours devoted to each category : A, B, C and R.
5. Now determine if your division of time corresponds to your objectives. If not, you should question the discrepancy between your priorities and your use of time and adjust your schedule accordingly.

SCHEDULE

Week of _____

to _____

19 _____

	MONDAY	TUESDAY	WEDNESDAY	THURSDAY	FRIDAY	SATURDAY	SUNDAY
07:00							
07:30							
08:00							
08:30							
09:00							
09:30							
10:00							
10:30							
11:00							
11:30							
12:00							
12:30							
13:00							
13:30							
14:00							
14:30							
15:00							
15:30							

	16:00	16:30	17:00	17:30	18:00	18:30	19:00	19:30	20:00	20:30	21:00	21:30	22:00	22:30	23:00	23:30

Certain management principles may help you make the changes needed. You want to modify your schedule but to do so you will undoubtedly have to act or react differently. Here are some guidelines:

1. MANAGING BY EXCEPTION

Managing by exception means delegating trivial or routine tasks to other resource people and only dealing with important tasks. For example, a student familiar with library research may prefer to use a computer to do this work for him. He thus saves time for studying or collating the information gathered. A mother who is going back to school can look for tasks that can be done by her children or her husband so she can successfully complete her studies without too much stress.

To achieve your priority goals more efficiently, review your daily activities to identify those which you can delegate to others: cleaners, subordinates, partners, etc.

2. DECIDE WHAT NOT TO DO

A good way to be sure of meeting your type A goals is to manage your time by deciding to eliminate certain activities. By refusing to do unimportant things, you can free time for achieving your type A objectives. This strategy will gradually teach you how to concentrate on your priorities.

3. SAY NO

Often it is difficult to reach your goals because of lack of resistance to environmental pressures. Knowing how to say "no" is an indispensable skill in conserving energy. Our education and courtesy standards often link saying "no" to an act of aggression or rejection. By always acting this way, however, you accumulate frustrations which cause feelings of emptiness, incompetence or depression. If you do not know how to resist the demands of those around you, you will never be able to manage your time in a way that lets you attain your goals.

Start right now to refuse projects that are not convenient for you. In difficult cases, think of intermediate solutions which will be profitable to both sides: compromise, discussion, setting common priorities and exchanging viewpoints.

If, in spite of adjustments to your schedules and applying good management principles, you find that you are still postponing your type A activities, perhaps you suffer a chronic or periodic procrastinatory tendency. Instead of reproaching yourself or resigning yourself willy-nilly to your fate, remember that stalling often accompanies difficult, complex or disagreeable tasks.In other words, when you like what you are doing and you know how to do it, you take the time to do it. Observe your behavior and you will notice that you put off disagreeable tasks and tasks whose complexity puts you off from the start. Let's look at some useful reactions to both cases.

If the task appears complex at first, here are a few suggestions to help you get started. A first possibility is called the Swiss-cheese technique — making holes in the task. Any complex or long task requires a series of activities of a minimal duration of 10 to 20 minutes which are inroads to achieving the task. Thus, instead of performing a type C activity, when your type A activity is furnishing your apartment, you can use a free period of 10 minutes to read a book on interior decorating. In this way, you have already broached the task unawares. After making several "holes," you will see that the original complexity has been considerably reduced and the task now seems reasonable. Before starting on a complex task, list all the activities which let you make "holes" in it: by knowing what they are, you will use more of your time for them instead of for type C tasks.

Another technique is to set aside five minutes a day to work on your project. Don't knock it. Five minutes, no more! Five minutes is so short that you can follow the rule without much effort. And who knows, it might give you the motivation to continue for another 10 minutes.

Some objectives are difficult to achieve because they are not well-planned. If this is so, take a sheet of paper and specify the different activities needed to complete your project. Be as detailed and concrete as possible to increase your chances of acting. Write up a contract and specify what you will do: "I've decided to get into shape; tomorrow I'll go to the bookstore on the corner and buy a book of exercises, etc." If you feel that you don't know how to plan an activity, imagine that a friend has asked your advice and list what suggestions you would make. This technique helps you discover your own resources.

Lack of information about a task can sometimes hinder its accomplishment. Only by reading relevant research on a thesis subject will you see all the elements that make it up. Getting information from books, specialists or even friends helps you better understand the why and the how of a task and makes it easier to do. Always take the precaution of organizing, classifying and condensing the information already gathered before collecting more.

Some stimuli can become restrictive and spur you to action. An open book on your night table or jogging shoes put in a strategic place can do this. Try to find restricting stimuli for the project you're planning. You can also take advantage of a mood to accomplish a type

A task. For example, you have to write a paper but you're in the mood to talk to friends. Find a friend with whom you can discuss your paper. Another way to make yourself act is to give yourself a little pep talk or to promise a friend that you will finish a project at a given time.

Once the work is underway, don't be surprised if your motivation decreases. Often, the stimuli must change to keep you motivated. You can rest or go on to another part of your daily schedule. For example, if you're tired of reading, stop and drink a glass of water or take notes on what you've read. The change may encourage you to persevere.

When you have to fill in your income-tax forms, make a business telephone call or ask for a postponement, you may often put off the chore until your back is against the wall. What should you do when you keep postponing a task because it is unpleasant? A useful strategy is to slow down the decision process and think of the three following aspects:

- The specifically unpleasant part or parts of the task. Doing this, you may find that you're afraid of part of it. Then you can reason with yourself or imagine the worst that could happen if you take the risk of doing what you're planning. You'll then see that your apprehensions are silly or exaggerated and react more realistically.
- The inconveniences of delaying. Take the time to identify the costs (material, physical or psychological) that you will have to pay if you do not do it.
- The advantages of getting it done. Centre on all the advantages related to accomplishing the task and imagine the pleasure you will feel.

At first, you may not succeed at slowing down the decision process and thus will still avoid doing the task. Admit to yourself that you have lost time even though you may have spent it on type B or type C activities. Better again: do nothing. Sit still and enjoy not doing what scares or displeases you. You will be surprised at the long-term results.

To sum up, remember two obvious facts that are often forgotten in time management. The first deals with material organization, the other with the psychological conditions of accomplishing a project.

The material conditions of carrying out a task must be planned from the first stages of implementing a project. So many people lose time through lack of organization. For example, they plan an evening of work and then realize that they don't have the materials needed. A few minutes or hours spent on organizing a task can avoid these useless and stressful wastes of time.

The psychological conditions in which you accomplish a task are as important as the material conditions. It's difficult to do what you want in life if you are depressed, tired or in poor mental or physical health. If there is a problem, don't hesitate to make up a problem-solving process and immediately correct the situation.

You now have a methodology for time management, but remember that learning is a process of trial-and-error in gradual and progressive steps. Learning to manage your time is no different. You will abandon the project if you expect to succeed at the first attempt. It's easy to label yourself "disorganized" but a lot more difficult to become a good time manager.

12. Physical exercise

The role of exercise in maintaining good physical condition only began to be perceived at the beginning of the century. Since then, there has been a boom in intensive physical-conditioning programs.

In spite of the efforts made, specialists quickly noticed that their advice was not being followed. Cardiac illnesses and obesity problems kept increasing and, in the '50s, it was realized that the problem had to be stated otherwise and a "witch hunt" against widespread myths about physical activity began. The average person was discouraged from taking part in training programs by these myths. They still exist today: there's "no gain without pain," you have to train intensively, sweat a lot, eat a lot of protein and, of course, jog because this is the ultimate in exercise.

Since the 1950s, simpler programs like the 5BX and 10BX have been developed in Canada to uproot these prejudices and show that good physical training is done at an individual's own pace, requires only the effort the body can give, and takes only a few minutes a day. The specialists say it is not even necessary to get into a program in order to be physically fit. Your daily activities can provide regular exercise. We will see how further on.

WHY EXERCISE?

Physical activity is a determining factor in keeping physically fit and thereby self-managing internal conditions of resistance to stress.

As well as improving physical condition, exercise helps concentration, improves sleep, gets rid of aggression that has no other outlet, gives a feeling of personal control and competence and provides a greater bodily awareness. Glasser talks about sports as a positive "drug." He shows that activities such as jogging reduce muscular tension and produce inner strength and mind-body harmony, essential elements in resistance to stress.

Exercise raises physical capacity to a level higher than the energy required for daily activities, and thus increases the ratio of work accomplished to energy expended. In other words, you get tired less quickly and have more energy for your free time or for tolerating daily stress.

Jean-Marc Brunet, a respected Quebec naturopath, writes:

"A healthy diet, fresh air, sound and refreshing sleep, sunshine, cleanliness and positive thinking are essential to longevity... But an even more important factor is physical activity of all kinds."

Paavo Airola, a well-known American dietitian, shares his opinion:

"Nutrition is the third most important factor in health. Exercise is the second. In fact, it's better to eat junk food and exercise strenuously than to eat healthily and do no exercise."

Modern life is sedentary. Work rarely requires strength or physical exercise. It's estimated that the average student remains seated for 15,000 hours between the first year of school and university. A professional is seated for 60,000 hours between the first year of work and retirement.

The effects of lack of exercise on muscular strength, joint flexibility, heart efficiency and circulation are well known.

Muscular strength is easily observable when carrying a heavy object or staying in shape after strenuous activity. Larger muscles not only aid blood circulation but use up more calories, even when at rest. For example, a 60-year-old man would have to run 6 miles a day to burn up the same number of calories as he did sitting down when he was younger. When not regularly exercised, muscles atrophy and lose their strength. There is even a muscle called the vastus internus, located in the knee, which will disappear in a few days if not exercised.

Deprived of exercise, tendons shorten and cause contraction of the joints which makes even simple movements such as turning or bending difficult. When these movements become difficult, people find all sorts of tricks to avoid them : lifting the foot to tie the shoe, sitting down instead of remaining standing, etc. By the fifties, or even before, the back is stooped, the shoulders rounded, the knees bent, etc. all because of joints stiffened by a lack of exercise. This is not merely a question of esthetics. Stiff joints affect all the body's functioning. A stooped back prevents the lungs from the full movement needed for good respiration.

The heart is a muscle. A healthy heart pumps blood easily and quickly from the venous system to the arterial system. Thus the heart must be exercised if it is to function normally; if not, its volume decreases and it becomes incapable of storing enough blood to create a strong muscular contraction. The efficiency of the blood oxygenation system is then considerably reduced.

Small arteries tend to close following lack of exercise, thereby increasing the risk of cardiac illnesses. Exercise keeps the blood vessels open so that if a major artery becomes blocked, the blood can detour through the smaller arteries.

An average adult's lungs contain six litres of air, of which only a fraction, around a half-litre when resting, is exchanged at each breath. Exercise increases the vital capacity of the lungs, that is, the rate of air that can be breathed out after taking the deepest breath possible, around four to five litres.

Hypokinetics studies of volunteer subjects or patients hospitalized after serious operations have showed that the resulting weakness depends in large part on physical inactivity. The body adapts rapidly to the activity demands made on it. Unlike a machine, the more it is used, the more fit it is.

To sum up, a sedentary lifestyle reduces useful muscle mass, impairs the oxygen transport system whether at rest or in motion and affects venous return performance. Lack of exercise also has several indirect consequences: it causes decalcification of the bones, increases the risks of obesity, hinders the normal functioning of digestion and elimination, and induces a number of disorders such as back pain, coronary illnesses, psychosomatic illnesses, aesthetic problems and greater accident-proneness.

WHAT IS YOUR OPTIMAL PHYSICAL CONDITION?

Several factors contribute to developing and maintaining physical fitness. Heredity is basic but illnesses, accidents and physical training can alter this.

Fluctuations in factors responsible for physical fitness and differences observed between men and women are 50% dependent on heredity. For example, a woman has only 60% of a man's physical strength and some people are born with the potential to become athletes just as some are potentially geniuses.

Hereditary potential is nonetheless modified by illness, accidents, environmental conditions, aging and physical training. Physical training can affect the efficiency of the oxygen delivery system to tissues, the percentage of body fat, muscular vigour, posture and pelvic position, all important variables in physical fitness. Intensive programs can modify the oxygen transport system by 40%, muscular strength by 100% and muscular stamina by up to 500%. They can also reduce body fat by 75%.

Unless you are already an athlete or are in top condition, you can always improve your physical fitness through various forms of physical conditioning. Always remember that you are the sole judge in this area and it's up to you to determine the goals you want and can reach.

ARE YOU FIT?

Being fit does not mean being an athlete but being able to meet the many demands of daily life and having enough energy in reserve to deal with sudden and unexpected stress. Morehouse describes the five conditions for minimum body upkeep as follows:

1. Moving the major joints in various ways to keep the body supple.
2. Standing up for at least two hours a day (not necessarily at one time) to help blood circulation and keep the skeleton in shape.
3. Lifting an unusually heavy weight for at least five seconds to maintain muscle strength.
4. Increasing heartbeats to 120 per minute for at least three minutes per day to exercise heart muscles.
5. Burning 300 calories a day in physical exercise to prevent obesity.

It's easy to see that all these conditions can be met in a normal day. The housewife who walks briskly to the grocery store, doesn't hesitate to bend and stretch to find something, carries the groceries home and then goes on to vacuum, make beds and dust meets all fitness requirements. In the same way, an office worker who runs his own errands rather than asking the secretary, remains standing when he could sit down, gets off the bus two stops ahead to walk the rest of the way and does odd jobs around the house can keep in shape even though his job is sedentary.

Nonetheless, because modern life offers so much inactivity, we have to think consciously about keeping fit and create exercise opportunities or get into a fitness program.

HOW TO EVALUATE
A PHYSICAL-FITNESS PROGRAM

A physical-fitness program should make muscles supple and strong, exercise the heart while respecting the person's initial condition and personal pace, decrease the percentage of body fat and improve ability to relax.

1. A good fitness program should have flexibility exercises.

   It takes two minutes and a half per day to maintain flexibility. The 10BX and 5BX programs begin with stretching exercises. Unless you have sports, artistic or meditative ambitions, these exercises or others like them will keep you supple.

2. A good fitness program should have exercises relating to muscular strength.

   Exercises to increase muscular strength make up a substantial part of any good fitness program.

3. A good fitness program should exercise the heart.

   It's commonly believed that strenuous exercise is needed to exercise the heart, but duration is most important. The exercise should be done continuously for at least two minutes and increase the heart rate to 110-120 beats per minute in order to exercise the heart properly. Running, for example, fulfills this condition — running in place, as in the 10BX and 5BX exercises, or jogging.

4. A good fitness program must respect the initial physical condition and personal pace.

   Heart rate must be considered as a guiding measure in a fitness program. A person in poor physical condition has muscles stronger than the heart and strenuous muscular effort will exhaust the heart. Even more so, people with heart problems must be sure to respect their personal rhythm.

Murray suggests the following procedure to determine physical condition and personal pace. The absolute maximum heart rate for a 20-year-old man in good condition, 200 beats per minute, is taken as the standard measure. From this figure, deduct your age and a handicap of 40 for poor physical condition, and you get the maximum heart rate to reach at the beginning of your training. If you are 35 years old, the rate will be 125 : 200 – (35 + 40). Then, gradually reduce your handicap by 1, from 40 to 39 and so on. If you are under 30, you can reduce your handicap to 0. Those over 30 will keep a residual handicap according to their age : 5 and less for those between 30 and 40, 15 and less between 40 and 50 and 20 for those over 50. In any case, remember that it is better to increase your cardiac rate to 110 or 120 beats per minute than to lower your handicap.

TWO FITNESS PROGRAMS FOR ORDINARY PEOPLE

1. 10BX and 5BX exercises.

The 10BX and 5BX programs, developed by the Royal Canadian Air Force, are simple, progressive, balanced, complete, personal and convenient. They do not require special equipment, take up little space and can easily be done at home in about 10 minutes a day. They increase muscular strength and stamina, maintain the body's suppleness and flexibility, and improve cardiovascular functioning.

The two programs consist of a daily routine of exercises increasing in difficulty up to the maximum point which varies according to age and sex. The 5BX program, designed for men, has five basic exercises that can be done in 11 minutes. The 10BX is designed for women and has 10 exercises that take 12 minutes.

The two programs have a certain number of stages and, from one stage to the next, the basic exercise is modified to require progressive effort. It is important to respect the overall time limit of 11 minutes for the 5BX and 12 for the 10BX, but the time allotted for individual exercises can be varied within this limit. The degree of physical ability is determined by your age group and, even though you may be tempted to progress quickly, it is strongly recommended that you follow the program stages. You will need six months or more of daily exercises to reach the degree indicated for your case but, once this level is reached, three sessions per week will be enough to keep you in shape. If you skip a day, go back to the previous level. And if you drop the program for a month or more, start again at the beginning.

2. Walking

Calling walking a physical-fitness program may seem strange. However, this activity is a complete physical exercise accessible to anyone, even people who have had heart attacks, and can be done many times a day. Walking is becoming a more and more popular sport. It's estimated that out of the 66 million Americans who exercise regularly, 46 million use walking as their sole method of keeping fit.

The effects of walking have been proved. This exercise, like jogging, improves cardiovascular functioning, reduces cholesterol levels and strengthens muscles.

With training, the heart rate can be reduced by seven beats a minute for a total of five million beats a year. And, unlike jogging, walking does not involve a risk of damage to the body.

There are other well-known effects of walking. Walking soothes insomnia, anxiety and nervous disorders without the side effects of tranquilizers or other drugs. It promotes calmness and reflection. Many great scientists and other thinkers walked regularly, among them Einstein, Freud and Thoreau who all used to walk three or four hours a day. Walking also improves physical condition and appearance by increasing energy expenditure and encouraging better posture and circulation. It helps get rid of back problems and obesity. In fact, several studies have shown that walking is the exercise that motivates the largest number of obese people to follow a physical-fitness program and that it is particularly effective in regaining and maintaining normal weight.

To get the maximum benefit from walking, specialists recommend an optimal muscular-tension level. Find this level as follows : First walk as you would normally to see your normal level of tension. Then increase this level to its maximum. Then reduce the tension until you become completely limp, almost to the point of falling down. Then slowly increase the tension so you are walking lightly and flexibly. When the quadriceps muscles in front are supple, your hips swing more and give a marked increase to the length of your stride. The ankles, knees and hips become shock absorbers. This additional cushion lets you raise your centre of gravity and avoid unnecessary movements. There are other not inconsiderable effects : your walk becomes more sensual and pleasant and helps eliminate the thigh widening known as "riding breeches" or "jodhpurs".

To encourage better posture and increase energy expenditure, throw out your chest while walking and swing your arms from side to side. Throwing out your chest improves pelvic swing and lengthens and strengthens abdominal muscles to support the movement. The back thigh muscles can then move the leg forward more easily while the lower back muscles will be relaxed rather than unnecessarily tense. The alternating movement of the arms helps the legs to stabilize the body.

Take advantage of the many daily opportunities for walking. Get into the habit of walking a little before taking the bus, going to the corner store on foot, climbing stairs rather than taking the elevator, etc. If you have no training, take a week to get used to it before walking more than fifteen minutes a day. Then gradually increase the time and pace.

Readers who want to practise a sport to keep fit should find out the specific effects of various sports activities. Remember that practising a sport generally requires good physical condition and you'll need preliminary training. Furthermore, each session of strenuous physical exercise requires warm-up exercises or you may get muscle cramps or even a heart attack.

13. Diet

To function properly, body cells must be supplied with the substances they need for their maintenance, functioning and reproduction. A good diet contains carbohydrates, fats, proteins, minerals and water. Only a balanced and varied diet can furnish all these elements.

Each nutritional element fulfills a special function. Carbohydrates and fat are mainly energy sources. Proteins serve especially for tissue formation. Vitamins are necessary for making enzymes, which play many roles in metabolism. Minerals are essential for the upkeep of several physiological processes, strengthening bones and maintaining cardiac, cerebral, muscular and nervous vigour. Water is the most important nutrient. Water is responsible for digestive, circulatory and excretory processes; it transports substances around the body; it is necessary for tissue formation and helps regulate body temperature.

The relationship between diet and stress is evident. An inappropriate diet stresses the body by preventing or hindering normal metabolism. In some cases, without external help such as food or medication to reestablish normal metabolism, poor eating habits can cause illnesses.

Did you know that...

- 60% of the leading causes of death in North America are linked to poor nutrition?
- Studies link the increase in the overall mortality rate, particularly from cardiovascular problems, to excess consumption of foods rich in saturated fat? Animal fat is saturated and 40 to 50% of the fats ingested in a day come from meats (among Canadian men and women between 20 and 39 years old).
- Breast and intestinal cancers are much more widespread in populations with high-fat diets?
- The most recent statistics show a sugar consumption of 112 pounds per year per person and, according to many researchers, this causes problems such as diabetes, cavities, depression, fatigue, hyperactivity, constipation, etc.?
- One Canadian in two is obese?
- There are many undernourishment problems in wealthy countries because of a lack of essential substances or an over-abundance of unhealthy foods?

The facts are inarguable but what foods must you eat to be healthy? There are so many contradictory slogans nowadays that it is difficult to get a coherent idea of the situation. Should you consume more Vitamin B-12, vegetarian products, sardines (DNA), etc.? Should you drink two quarts of water a day or avoid liquids so you don't eliminate your mineral salts?

Even the experts disagree. Paavo Airola, a biochemist, and Whitaker, a doctor, denounce the myth of a diet high in protein and low in carbohydrates. On the other hand, Atkins, a doctor, recommends that overweight people should avoid carbohydrates in particular. Roger Williams, a biochemist, thinks the vitamin doses recommended by dietitians are too low and advises taking more. Other specialists recommend vegetarian, lacto-ovo-vegetarian [1] or all-natural diets to reduce problems of obesity, cholesterol or food poisoning. Some even suggest fasting as a detoxification and regeneration cure.

We've all heard that coffee should be avoided, that sugar is pure poison, that food colorings are carcinogenic and that salt causes high blood pressure. How can we place our faith in these opinions when taboo foods and miracle foods vary so much from one suggested diet to the other?

A closer look shows that, despite considerable divergences of opinion, most specialists agree on a group of ideas and facts. Rationally, it would seem that there is little risk in trusting them, given the proofs they put forward.

The currently accepted ideas in the dietary area are very well summarized in the Quebec Food Guide, published by the Quebec government.

"We realize today that we over-eat, without proper judgment. The number of modern illnesses (obesity, cardiovascular illnesses, etc.) could be greatly reduced if we adopted better eating habits." [2]

---

1. A vegetarian diet uses only foods of vegetable origin while a lacto-ovo-vegetarian diet forbids meats but allows some animal products such eggs and cheese.

2. Denis Lazure, Quebec Minister of Social Affairs.

Specialists have identified many unhealthy eating habits in modern nutrition. They denounce overconsumption : we eat too much. They also point to imbalances in our choice of foods. We consume too much sugar, fat, alcohol and salt when we would benefit greatly from a more varied diet and eating more fruits, vegetables and high-fibre foods.

What must we eat to be healthy ? The Canada Food Guide suggests a program based on daily nutritional needs, using Canadian nutritional standards. It recommends a choice of foods as well as the proportions needed. According to your age, you must consume certain proportions of food from the four food groups : milk and dairy products, bread and cereals, fruits and vegetables, and meat and meat substitutes.

By following the guide, each day you will absorb the substances needed for normal body functioning. Milk and dairy products supply calcium, Vitamins A, B and D and proteins. Bread and cereals are excellent sources of iron and Vitamin B. If you choose whole grains (bread and cereals made from unrefined products) you will also get high-fibre substances. Fruits and vegetables supply Vitamins A and C as well as iron. Meats and meat substitutes such as nuts and cheese fill protein needs.

Some recommendations also help guide the choice and preparation of foods within each food group. In the "milk and dairy products" group, the guide advises drinking milk or eating milk-based cooked foods since there are few easily available sources of Vitamin D.

Canada's Food Guide

Eat a variety of foods from each group every day

milk and milk products

children up to
years 2-3 servings
dolescents 3-4 servings
egnant and nursing
omen 3-4 servings
dults 2 servings

**meat, fish, poultry and alternates
2 servings**

**breads and cereals
3-5 servings**

hole grain or enriched

**fruits and vegetables
4-5 servings**

Include at least two vegetables.

Health and Welfare
Canada

Santé et Bien-être social
Canada

© Minister of Supply and Services Canada 1983
Cat. No. H58-32/1983-2E

Canadä

Canada's Food Guide

Variety

Choose different kinds of foods from within each group in appropriate numbers of servings and portion sizes.

Energy Balance

Needs vary with age, sex and activity. Balance energy intake from foods with energy output from physical activity to control weight. Foods selected according to the Guide can supply 4000 – 6000 kJ (kilojoules) (1000 – 1400 kilocalories). For additional energy, increase the number and size of servings from the various food groups and/or add other foods.

Moderation

Select and prepare foods with limited amounts of fat, sugar and salt. If alcohol is consumed, use limited amounts.

milk and milk products

Children up to 11 years — 2-3 servings
Adolescents — 3-4 servings
Pregnant and nursing women — 3-4 servings
Adults — 2 servings

Skim, 2%, whole, buttermilk, reconstituted dry or evaporated milk may be used as a beverage or as the main ingredient in other foods. Cheese may also be chosen.

Some examples of one serving
250 mL (1 cup) milk
175 mL (¾ cup) yoghurt
45 g (1½ ounces) cheddar or process cheese

In addition, a supplement of vitamin D is recommended when milk is consumed which does not contain added vitamin D.

meat, fish, poultry and alternates
2 servings

Some examples of one serving
60 to 90 g (2–3 ounces) cooked lean meat, fish, poultry or liver
60 mL (4 tablespoons) peanut butter
250 mL (1 cup) cooked dried peas, beans or lentils
125 mL (½ cup) nuts or seeds
60 g (2 ounces) cheddar cheese
125 mL (½ cup) cottage cheese
2 eggs

breads and cereals
3-5 servings

whole grain or enriched. Whole grain products are recommended.

Some examples of one serving
1 slice bread
125 mL (½ cup) cooked cereal
175 mL (¾ cup) ready-to-eat cereal
1 roll or muffin
125 to 175 mL (½ – ¾ cup) cooked rice, macaroni, spaghetti or noodles
½ hamburger or wiener bun

fruits and vegetables
4-5 servings

Include at least two vegetables.

Choose a variety of both vegetables and fruits — cooked, raw or their juices. Include yellow, green or green leafy vegetables.

Some examples of one serving
125 mL (½ cup) vegetables or fruits – fresh, frozen or canned
125 mL (½ cup) juice – fresh, frozen or canned
1 medium-sized potato, carrot, tomato, peach, apple, orange or banana

Yogurt and cheese do not contain Vitamin D but like milk they are excellent sources of calcium. Also, butter, whipped cream, sour cream and cream cheeses are not considered as adequate portions in this food group because of their high fat and low calcium content.

Whole-grain products are preferable to refined products because the latter lose a large part of their nutritional value in the refining process. Whole-grain products contain the alimentary fibres needed for good intestinal functioning and are excellent sources of iron and vitamins. If refined products are used, they should be enriched while being processed. In Canada, white flour must be enriched with iron, thiamin, riboflavin and niacin, but the contents of pasta and cereals are not regulated.

Fruits and vegetables provide the Vitamin A and C we need and are a good source of iron. To preserve all their nutritional value, they should be consumed fresh and raw, if possible, or barely cooked, preferably steamed. This is because Vitamins A and C and dietary fibre contained in fruits and vegetables are destroyed or lost when exposed to air or water or by prolonged cooking.

One of the goals of Quebec's nutritional policy is to reduce the fat content of our diet by 20%. In Canada, 40 to 50% of all fat ingested daily by adults (men and women between 20 and 39 years old) comes from meat, according to Nutrition Canada. While meat supplies protein, the guide recommends limiting daily portions to four or six ounces and using lean meats, fish or vegetable substitutes such as legumes, nuts and grains. Cheese is also a good source of protein but needs to be accompanied by green vegetables or bread to make up for its low iron content. Eggs, consumed in moderate quantities because of their high cholesterol content, can also be good meat substitutes.

Vegetarian diets are more and more popular nowadays. Although you can be healthy without them, they are nutritionally adequate. In order for the body to use them properly, certain rules of combining proteins must be followed. Legumes or nuts and seeds should be eaten with grains, or legumes with nuts and seeds. Grains can also be combined with dairy products to provide more protein. There are apparently many advantages to a vegetarian diet : fewer obesity problems, lower cholesterol, less osteoporosis and easier intestinal functioning. Also, vegetable products are a money-saving substitute for meats.

How many calories a day are needed for good health ? The number of calories which will maintain your ideal weight. For example, if your ideal weight is 70 kilos and you remain at that level by eating 2,000 calories a day, that is the number of calories you need daily. The answer varies with the individual : it depends on your age, your energy expenditure and your metabolism. In general, however, in Canada, men from 19 years old to 65 years old respectively require 3,000 to 2,300 calories per day and women from 19 to 65, require 2,100 to 1,800.

Obesity is such a widespread problem today that we should emphasize the importance of maintaining a weight suitable to the body's proper functioning. Did you know that the average Quebec man between 20 and 39 years old consumes 400 excess calories every day and Quebec women of the same age exceed the acceptable standard by 100 calories ? Consult table 8 to find out your ideal weight and, if necessary, take corrective measures.

A) Ideal weight for men of 25 and over

HEIGHT With shoes, 1-inch heels FEET	INCHES	SMALL FRAME	MEDIUM FRAME	LARGE FRAME
5	2	112–120	118–129	126–141
5	3	115–123	121–133	129–144
5	4	118–126	124–136	132–148
5	5	121–129	127–139	135–152
5	6	124–133	130–143	138–156
5	7	128–137	134–147	142–161
5	8	132–141	138–152	147–166
5	9	136–145	142–156	151–170
5	10	140–150	146–160	155–174
5	11	144–154	150–165	159–179
6	0	148–158	154–170	164–184
6	1	152–162	158–175	168–189
6	2	156–167	162–180	173–194
6	3	160–171	167–185	178–199
6	4	164–175	172–190	182–204

B) Ideal weight for women of 25 and over

HEIGHT With shoes, 2-inch heels FEET	INCHES	SMALL FRAME	MEDIUM FRAME	LARGE FRAME
4	10	92– 98	96–107	104–119
4	11	94–101	98–110	106–122
5	0	96–104	101–113	109–125
5	1	99–107	104–116	112–128
5	2	102–110	107–119	115–131
5	3	105–113	110–122	118–134
5	4	108–116	113–126	121–138
5	5	111–119	116–130	125–142
5	6	114–123	120–135	129–146
5	7	118–127	124–139	133–150
5	8	122–131	128–143	137–154
5	9	126–135	132–147	141–158
5	10	130–140	136–151	145–163
5	11	134–144	140–155	149–168
6	0	138–148	144–159	153–173

For girls between 18 and 25, subtract one pound for each year under 25.

1. Table 8 from Metropolitan Life Insurance, 1959.

DANGEROUS FOODS

Many studies show that some foods should be consumed in moderation or they will harm the body, because they destroy tissues or cause metabolic imbalances. Dangerous foods are sugar, fat, caffeine, alcohol, salt and processed products.

The question of the harmfulness of certain foods must be treated carefully. Medicine evolves rapidly. Some facts are well known, others less. We know that alcohol can cause cirrhosis of the liver. However, the cause-and-effect relationships have not been clearly established for some foods such as sugar and fats. A scientific demonstration can be difficult. How do you verify, for example, that your almost chronic tiredness comes from excessive sugar consumption? What the specialists say about food should be taken with a grain of salt.

TABLE 9[1]

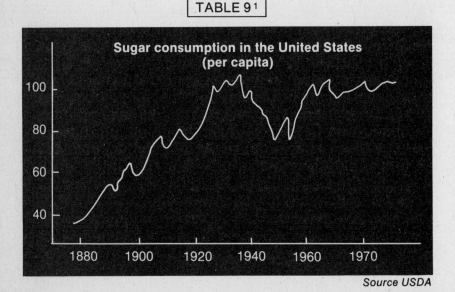

Source USDA

---

1. Table taken from M.F. Jacobson (1974).

SUGAR

Sugar consumption per capita increases every year. In the United States, it went from around 35 pounds per person in 1880 to about 100 pounds in 1970 (see Table 9). In Canada, sugar consumption was 112 pounds per person in 1980 and, according to statistics, Quebecers consume more than the national average.

Added sugar is so common in commercial food products that it is difficult to avoid in a modern diet. For example, added sugar accounts for 87% of the calories in a soft drink, 88% in Jell-O and 65% in a Del Monte fruit salad. Sugar is even added to soups, stews and salad dressings.

We know that sugar abuse promotes cavities and obesity and, for these reasons alone, it is strongly recommended that sugar use be limited in all its forms (sucrose, honey, maple syrup, etc.). But more and more studies link sugar abuse to hypoglycemia and as this research is less well known, we'll talk about it in more detail.

Sugar is the prime source of energy for all body cells, especially brain cells which are nourished by it alone. Sugar comes mainly from carbohydrates and glycogen. Carbohydrates are present in sweet and starchy foods and in cellulose; that is, in desserts, bread, pasta, fruits and vegetables. Gastric juices transform these carbohydrates into simple sugar called glucose. Part of the glucose is used as fuel by brain tissue, the nervous system and the muscles. Another part is transformed into glycogen and stored in the liver and the muscles: the excess is changed into fat and stocked in adipose tissue as an energy reserve.

In order for the body to function properly, the level of glucose in the blood should remain below a certain level. Hormones serve to maintain this balance. Insulin reduces the glucose level when it is too high; glucagon and adrenalin increase it when it is too low. Glucagon is secreted by the pancreas under the influence of cortin and cortisone, hormones manufactured in the adrenal cortex. When the organism undergoes stress, adrenalin performs functions similar to those of glucagon.

If insulin secretion or action is insufficient, the process of transforming glucose into glycogen will be affected, and the blood will contain too much sugar, creating a risk of diabetes. Conversely, if the concentration of sugar in the blood supply to the brain is too low, hypoglycemia results and the danger triggers a stress response, causing a discharge of adrenalin which acts on the liver to increase the blood sugar level. Note that several hormones increase the level of blood sugar but insulin is the only hormone that can decrease it. For this reason, the pancreas should treated with care to ensure its proper functioning.

Recent statistics show that diabetes is the third leading cause of death in North America. Hypoglycemia is not as well known an illness and specialists do not agree on its frequency. Some say one person out of 1,000 suffers from it, while others believe that 50% of the population is affected to some degree.

To understand what hypoglycemia is, let's look more closely at the effect of carbohydrates on the level of glucose in the blood. Ingesting carbohydrates increases the blood glucose level. The increase is more or less sudden depending on whether simple sugars are involved, which are easily digested, or complex sugars, which require several hours of digestion. Everyone is familiar enough with the energizing effect of a chocolate bar to know how instantaneous the effect of some carbohydrates can be. However, the metabolic processes do not stop there. The pancreas will react to the increase in the glucose level by producing insulin to transform the glucose into glycogen and reestablish a normal blood

sugar concentration. The more carbohydrates are consumed in the form of simple sugars, the more this decrease
is sudden and more likely to cause hypoglycemia.

The first symptoms of hypoglycemia are fatigue and
sleepiness. The person affected becomes nervous, irritable, smokes a cigarette, has a coffee or a snack. If the
correction of the blood glucose level does not occur
normally, more alarming symptoms may appear: they
vary depending on the speed of the decrease and the
magnitude of the corresponding stress reaction. If the
sugar concentration decreases slowly over several hours,
there may be vision problems, headaches, mental confusion and, possibly, coma.

If the decrease is rapid, the more frequent symptoms
are those which accompany an increase in adrenalin
secretion and these new symptoms such as sweating,
hunger, rapid heartbeat, trembling and anxiety are super-
imposed on the preceding ones. If the sugar level is not
corrected, nervous problems may appear: mood swings,
depression, hallucinations, motor problems and psychotic
symptoms.

CAFFEINE

Caffeine, contained in coffee, tea, soft drinks and
some chocolate products, has the same effect on the
organism as sugar. It activates the adrenal cortex,
increasing the level of blood glucose and immediately
boosting energy. In a short time, however, this increase
in the glucose level will be corrected as soon as the
blood reaches the pancreas and the ensuing decrease in

blood glucose will show up as a new feeling of fatigue. This causes a craving for a new food stimulant : a second coffee, a soft drink, pastry, etc. It is not advisable to consume large amounts of caffeine.

ALCOHOL

Alcohol is often appreciated for its euphoric and temporarily stimulating effects. Although its effects can be pleasant and, in the short term, can even help in stressful situations, alcohol causes well-known harmful effects : physical and psychological addiction, liver, heart, stomach and nervous-system disorders, psychoses and fatal accidents. Did you know that Quebec ranks third in the industrialized world for the percentage of alcoholics ?

Alcohol is dangerous in many ways. It contains about 70 calories an ounce and thus can satisfy the body's energy needs. But as these are empty calories, nutritional deficiencies are inevitable if alcohol is consumed to the detriment of other essential foods. Even if the diet is otherwise balanced, excessive consumption of alcohol not only increases the number of calories ingested but disturbs all body functions from muscle contractions to thinking processes.

Alcohol anesthetizes the central nervous system so the hypothalamus can no longer recognize danger and trigger the adrenalin secretion characteristic of the stress response. The danger may be internal, like a decrease in blood sugar, or external, like an icy road in the middle of the night. In both cases, the drunk person does not react normally to stress. But the real danger does not disappear and can result in illness and accidents.

Psychological dependence on alcohol, as on any other drug, is easy to understand. Unless other responses are learned or danger is perceived differently, drinking quickly becomes a habitual reaction to the stress signal.

SALT

Salt is a seasoning we use too much. While the body's daily needs for salt are 200 milligrams, the average consumption varies between 7 and 30 grams per day. This level is easily reached when you consider that a cup of Lipton soup contains 1 gram, three strips of bacon, 630 mg. and a 2-ounce bologna sausage, 525 mg.

Recent studies indicate a relationship between eating too much salt and arterial hypertension. Northern Japanese eat a large amount of salted foods and 40% have high blood pressure while only half as many southern Japanese, who eat half as much salt, have this problem. Studies show that Greenland Eskimos, Kenyan nomads, Central and South American Indians and the inhabitants of New Guinea and the Solomon Islands, who eat very little salt, rarely suffer from high blood pressure. Laboratory research shows the same tendencies. In all animal species, excessive and lasting ingestion of salt increases blood pressure.

It seems, however, that an innate or hereditary predisposition must exist for the harmful effects of salt to appear. Mayer has shown that the arterial tension of persons suffering from high blood pressure is inversely proportional to the ability of their red blood cells to excrete sodium.

Studies on preventing hypertension are conclusive: most cases of high blood pressure can be improved or cured by restricting salt in the diet.

FATS

Fats make an important contribution to our diet. They supply a concentrated energy source, help absorption of Vitamins A, D, E and K, increase the flavour of food and give us a feeling of satiety.

According to present statistics, however, fats make up too much of our total food consumption — around 40%. In addition, this percentage is mainly saturated fatty acids. Saturated fatty acids are mostly of animal origin. They are found in meats, unskimmed dairy products and in some oils and margarines as well as in chocolate.

Three fatty acids known as Vitamin F are essential to the body which cannot manufacture them. These are non-saturated fatty acids needed for growth, good cardiac, arterial and nervous-system functioning, and skin and tissue health. These acids are also believed to play a part in transporting and using cholesterol.

Cholesterol is a lipid needed for health. It is a normal component of most body tissue. It is also needed for forming hormones, Vitamin D and bile. Cholesterol can be stored in the body if it is not used. Although studies are not conclusive, it seems that the consumption of saturated fatty acids almost always coincides with a high blood cholesterol level, which promotes arteriosclerosis.

To reduce your blood cholesterol level, you should use polyunsaturated fats such as sunflower, corn, saffron and soya oils and regularly substitute fish for meat. It should be noted that frying as well as the hydrogenation process frequently used in the extraction of commercial oils saturate the fatty acid molecule. It is important, therefore, to avoid fried foods and to choose cold-pressed oils from among those mentioned above.

PROCESSED FOOD PRODUCTS

To preserve foods and help market them, the food industry processes more and more basic foods by refining them and adding preservatives and colorings. Grains, rice and pasta are refined, destroying their high fibre, vitamin and natural enzyme content. Also, the production of artificial food colorings went from around 300,000 pounds in 1940 to more than four million pounds in 1970. Studies regularly expose the carcinogenic nature of certain chemical additives but once they are taken off the market, they are — some researchers say — replaced by equally harmful products.

Although specialists agree on the importance of eating fresh foods and recommend whole grains, they are far from agreeing about processed foods. Some say we are needlessly alarmed. Their argument is that all foods are "chemical" and government controls ensure the quality of products put on the market. In their opinion, we should be more concerned about the effects of overeating, lack of exercise, alcohol abuse and tobacco on health than about the negligible effects of the colorings and preservatives added to food.

Natural-food exponents deplore the damaging effects of modern eating habits. Many studies link consumption of refined products and colorings to physical and psychological illnesses. A study done in schools showed that eliminating refined products and colorings significantly reduced hyperactivity problems among students.

The controversy prevents our taking a definitive stand on the subject. For now, it's perhaps better to be prudent and, insofar as possible, choose fresh, natural or enriched products over processed products without getting carried away and buying nothing but expensive "health foods."

14. Relaxation methods

There are many daily stress situations. Whether writing an exam, finishing a job, finishing a training period, taking a course, hearing bad news, etc., our bodies are subjected to the stress of everyday life. The resulting physical or psychological tension manifests itself in the body's muscular system. Fortunately, perhaps, because it is easier to relax the muscles than the mind. Indeed, muscular relaxation techniques are simple and their effectiveness in reducing stress has been known for a long time.

Relaxation has many positive effects: a 10 to 20% reduction of arterial tension, significant decrease in heartbeat, a 30 to 60% decrease in breathing frequency, fuller inhalations and exhalations, relaxing of general muscle tension and a reduction in visual and auditory perception causing a state similar to that observed during sleep.

There are several proven methods of relaxation. We have chosen to talk about meditation, Jacobson's progressive relaxation, Bertherat's warm-ups and three types of relaxation breaks. The variety of these techniques will let you make a judicious choice, taking into account the available time, your personality and your lifestyle.

MEDITATION

Meditation is universally recognized for its beneficial effects on the body. For those who practise it, it has become the favorite way of relaxation, contemplation and inner revitalization.

Meditation consists of centering your attention during a specific period of time on a particular thing or subject and pulling yourself back constantly, gently but firmly, to this. Several techniques for reaching this goal have been invented over time. Some, like Krishnamurti, draw their meditative subjects from the intellectual sphere; others, such as the great Christian mystics, preferred the realm of emotions. Hatha Yoga, Tai Chi or, more contemporarily, the Alexander method, go the corporal route while Aikido or the Zen art of archery choose the way of action. No technique is better than another; it remains a personal choice based on where the individual feels strongest and safest.

The physical effects of meditation are grouped around two main results: a physiological state of deep relaxation and a mental state of awakening and alertness. The body's relaxed state during meditation manifests itself in a slowed metabolism, a low heartbeat rate, a decrease in breathing rate and volume, an increase in skin resistance to a moderate electric current and an increase in alpha waves. But contrary to sleep, where the same characteristics are found, the meditative state increases the brain's capacity for alertness and stimulation. Although there is no scientific proof, it is believed that this effect is due to the very activity of meditation, focusing and centering on a single thing at a time.

Psychologically, meditation leads in time to a new way of perceiving reality. Normally, reality is seen and known through the intellect, which uses classes and categories to identify and distinguish things. Meditation encourages a different mode of knowledge. The unique nature of each thing is grasped. It is difficult to define this mode of understanding the real with the logical categories we ordinarily use. An analogy may make it clearer: when you are in love, the loved one is unique and irreplaceable. Meditation allows us to get back in touch with a part of ourselves that is often lost and from this comes an increase in vitality and a greater ability to form deep relationships and to love.

Meditation also increases personal competence and renews our enthusiasm for daily life. These effects arise from the activity itself. As a constant and deliberate effort to draw one's attention, gently but with discipline, to the chosen subject, meditation strengthens concentration, mind power and perseverance in the pursuit of one's goals.

To begin meditating, first choose a quiet place where you will not be disturbed. Choose an opportune time. It is suggested that meditating should done at a fixed time in order to develop the habit and ensure regularity — for example, upon rising, coming home from work or at bedtime. Wait two hours after a meal before meditating because digestion apparently affects the process. Remove any tight clothing, get into a comfortable position and be sure the room is warm since your metabolism will slow down during the meditative process. Beginners are recommended to practise daily for from fifteen to twenty minutes.

These conditions met, you now have to decide on a type of meditation and centre yourself on the meditative subject so that you will be completely focused on it and not be conscious of anything else. In other words, the meditative subject will fill your entire field of consciousness. Naturally, you will often feel your attention wandering during this exercise. When you realize this, pull yourself back gently, without self-criticism, to the meditative subject.

Out of the many available, we will offer you two kinds of meditation for beginners. Choose the one that suits you better and don't hesitate to experiment to find one that will be more adaptable to your needs.

The Tibetan method of concentrating on your breathing consists of observing the movements of inhaling and exhaling. Although this is simple, its very simplicity makes it difficult. Some people suggest counting breaths (count 1 at the first exhalation, 2 at the next and so on, up to 4, and then start again) or to tell yourself mentally that you are inhaling at each inhalation and exhaling at each exhalation.

Meditating with a mantra is the most widespread method in the western world. You repeat a word or a sentence called a mantra. In the Hindu language, this word designates a sound, word or sentence whose consonance acts as a relaxant on the entire mind and body. After a few minutes of preparation, let your thoughts drift slowly without trying to concentrate until your mind is gently swayed by the sound of the mantra which you repeat without emphasis. The transcendental meditation movement claims that each mantra must be strictly personal and one should never divulge it to a third person. Yet, according to Delauniere and Gagnon, the TM movement has only sixteen mantras that instructors give out according to age group. Thus it is not necessary to spend money to know "your" mantra. You can choose the word "peace," "hallelujah," "shirim," "hirim" or whatever and proceed as we explained above to benefit fully from this type of meditation.

To check that the type of meditation chosen suits you, despite the difficulties inherent in the process, ask yourself after each meditation period if you have a greater sense of well-being. Also remind yourself that only regularity and perseverance can bring you the beneficial effects already mentioned.

JACOBSON'S PROGRESSIVE RELAXATION

Jacobson's progressive relaxation is a particularly effective technique. It not only brings immediate muscular relaxation but also teaches you how to relax. After one period of training, it can be used just about anywhere.

This method consists of a series of exercises which require tensing specific muscles, then relaxing the tension completely. You must centre on the tense state and the relaxed state so you can easily identify them and learn to recognize them. Immediately after being tensed, a muscle tends to loosen up more than usual which gives very pleasant sensations of deep muscle relaxation. Mahoney reports that this experience is comparable to taking a very hot bath after strenuous physical exercise. This shows the power of this very simple exercise. Furthermore, eventually you will learn to detect tension without contracting the muscles and after only a few practice sessions, most people develop the ability to reduce tension by simply concentrating on the more agreeable sensation of relaxation.

Laboratory tests have shown that these exercises reduce muscular tension and learning to relax can help solve problems such as insomnia or phobias.

To learn Jacobson's progressive relaxation, it is essential to identify the groups of muscles involved, know the corresponding movements of contraction and relaxation, and follow the order in which the activities are done.

Proceed as follows:

1. Read item 1 in Table 10.
2. Concentrate on the muscle group named.
3. Gradually make the tensing movement suggested.
4. Hold the tension for a few seconds.
5. Gradually relax the muscles.
6. Concentrate on the relaxation.
7. Go on to the next item, repeat steps 2 to 6 and continue up to the last item.

TABLE 10[1]

**Relaxation: Muscle groups
and corresponding movements.**

Muscle groups	Corresponding movements
1. Left hand	Make a fist and bend it back toward forearm.
2. Left arm	Make a fist and bend forearm back until hand touches shoulder.
3. Right hand	Repeat left hand exercise.
4. Right arm	Repeat left arm exercise.
5. Forehead	Raise eyebrows to crease forehead.
6. Eyes and lids	Close eyes as tightly as possible.
7. Mouth and jaw	Smile very widely and then open mouth wide, pressing down as if an object under the jaw were resisting
8. Tongue	Bring tip of tongue to where teeth meet the palate and without curling it, press on the palate.
9. Neck	Bend head forward and tuck chin under.

1. Table adapted from Francine Boucher, Jacqueline Avard.

10. Shoulders	Place arms at chest height, bring shoulders back as if shoulder blades were going to touch and while pointing elbows down, lower shoulders as much as possible.
11. Chest and abdomen	While inhaling, contract chest inward. Exhale and breathe normally, then push chest outward. Exhale and breathe normally.
12. Left thigh	Raise leg and point foot forward.
13. Left calf and foot	Raise leg, first point foot forward while lightly flexing toes, then point foot towards face. After holding the tension, rotate ankle several times and bring foot back to normal position.
14. Right thigh	Repeat left thigh exercise.
15. Right calf	Repeat left calf and foot exercise.

To help you learn, record the following text from a relaxation session on a cassette, carefully following these rules:

1. *Be sure the place is quiet and background noise is eliminated.*

2. *Read the text in a very firm tone when you have to contract or flex a muscle and a soft, calm voice when you have to relax or loosen a muscle.*

3. *Pause for several seconds each time the text indicates a break.*

4. *Take 15 to 20 minutes to record the session.*

"In several minutes you will have to practise your relaxation exercise. Sit in a relaxed position in a comfortable armchair, hands resting on the arms, feet flat on the ground. Close your eyes. Breathe calmly and regularly.

"Now concentrate on your left hand... Slowly, very slowly contract the muscles of your left hand... feel the tension... and gradually, completely relax your left hand... Concentrate on the difference between the tense state and the relaxed state of your left hand.

"Now turn your attention to your left arm... Slowly tighten the muscles... feel the tension... and slowly, relax your left arm...

"Concentrate now on the right hand... Gradually contract the muscles... feel the tension in all your hand and... slowly, completely relax the muscles.

---

1. Text adapted from Francine Boucher, Jacqueline Avard.

"Turn your attention to your right arm... Slowly contract the right arm... feel the tension invade the muscles of your right arm... centre on the tension... and slowly relax your right arm. Concentrate on the difference between the tension and the relaxation in your right arm.

"Concentrate now on the muscles of your forehead... contract your forehead muscles... feel the tension... and very gradually, release the tension.

"Turn your attention to your eye and eyelid areas... Slowly, contract this area... concentrate on the tension and, very gradually, begin to loosen the muscles... slowly... relax.

"Concentrate now on your jaw and mouth area. Contract the muscles... centre on the tension... and loosen up completely... relax.

"Now concentrate on your tongue. Contract the muscles... feel the tension... then, slowly, loosen the muscles.

"Concentrate now on relaxing the face muscles — the forehead, the eyes, the jaw, the mouth and the tongue.

"Now shift your attention to your neck. Gradually, contract the muscles of the neck... feel the tension... then slowly... relax the neck muscles.

"Move on to your shoulders... Tighten the muscles... concentrate on the tension... and, gradually, completely relax your shoulders.

"Concentrate now on the chest and abdomen area... First pull in your chest... feel the tension... and, slowly, relax the muscles... Breathe calmly and regularly... Now push your chest outward... centre on the tension... and, gradually, loosen the muscles, relax.

"Concentrate on your breathing: inhale... exhale... slowly, regularly... inhale... exhale...

"Concentrate on relaxing your upper body: your hands, arms, face muscles, neck, shoulders, chest and abdomen.

165

"Turn your attention to your left thigh now. Slowly, flex the muscles... feel the tension... and, gradually, completely loosen your left thigh... relax.

"Concentrate now on your left foot and calf... Gradually contract the muscles... feel the tension... and slowly relax the muscles.

"Now move on to your right thigh. Slowly tighten your right thigh... centre on the tension... and, very slowly, loosen the muscles, relax.

"Concentrate now on your right foot and calf. Gradually tighten the muscles... feel the tension... and, very slowly, gradually relax the foot and calf.

"Now feel the relaxation in your entire body: hands, arms, face muscles, neck, shoulders, chest, abdomen, legs and feet.

"I'm now going to count backwards from 4 to 1. At 4, you will move your fingers, at 3, your shoulders, at 2, your feet and at 1, you will open your eyes. 4... 3... 2... 1."

Since relaxation must be learned, the more often you practise, the more rapidly you will master the technique. We suggest the following stages. First practise twice a day, lying or seated and using the cassette. Be sure one of these practises is at bedtime. Also, during the day try to detect the times when you feel tense. This stage over, practice without using the cassette and, on occasion, only do the movements which correspond to the usual tension areas, linking the sensation of relaxation to the verbal key "relaxed" or "calm." Finally, train yourself to use the verbal key as often as possible to help yourself relax in daily situations as soon as you feel tense and, at the same time, concentrate on your breathing.

As you will see after practising a while, relaxing lets you replace an anxiety state with muscular relaxation. You may be familiar with other anxiety symptoms, such as nausea, sweating, shaky legs or headaches but these reactions are usually preceded or accompanied by muscular tension. If you manage to completely relax, the other physiological reactions will probably disappear.

BERTHERAT'S WARM-UPS

With a more humanist orientation than Jacobson, Bertherat proposes listening to one's body to relax and be physically and mentally fit. In her book, "The Body Has Its Reasons," she gives a series of exercises she calls warm-ups. As the word indicates, these are not physical exercises in the usual sense but positions or manipulations which help relax the body without effort or strain. When you do these exercises, you won't be surprised by Bertherat's calling them anti-gymnastics.

Bertherat recommends doing warm-ups while paying attention to one's physical sensations rather than the performance itself. In other words, don't try to "succeed;" the performance is less important than the process. It might be important to "fail" at a warm-up to understand the body's messages better.

We will give you ten warm-ups. They involve the principal muscles of the body. They are simple to do, but remember, they must be done gently and slowly without straining yourself. With practice, you'll be able to do them correctly.

Bertherat's exercises have been recorded on cassette and you may want to find them to make the process easier. Bertherat recommends observing the effects of each warm-up immediately after doing it : you will observe that these effects spread out over the half of the body corresponding to the muscle put in action.

WARM-UPS

1. *All the body*

Remove your belt or any other tight clothing. Lie on your back. Leave your arms at your sides, palms turned upwards, and relax your feet. Close your eyes. Remain silent. Without doing anything else and, even if you don't feel comfortable, observe which parts of your body are against the floor: heels, calves, buttocks, pelvis, sacrum, back, vertebrae, shoulders, head.

Pay attention to your jaw. If it is clenched, try to relax it. Let your tongue go limp in your mouth. Continue this as long as you wish.

2. *Feet*

This is work on the feet. You need a sponge ball about the size of a mandarin orange. While standing, place your right foot on the ball on the floor. Then gently massage the bottom of your foot with the ball. Massage the bottoms of all your toes, the ball of the foot, the instep and the heel. Don't turn your toes upward. Massage in small circles, gently and systematically, all over the bottom of the foot. If some parts of the foot are painful, be more gentle. To feel the immediate effects of this exercise, lie down and compare feelings in both sides of your body.

3. *Feet*

For this warm-up, which is also work on the foot, seat yourself comfortably on the ground. Place your right foot on your outstretched left leg. Take the large toe of your right foot in one hand and the rest of the foot in the other. Pull gently on the large toe, turning it slightly, as if you were screwing it on, then unscrew it. Do the same thing with your other toes. Pull and turn the toe from the base. Each of your toes corresponds to a given zone of your spinal column.

Now bend your right leg, raise your right foot, keeping your toes straight. Take the right large toe in one hand and, with the other, move the other toes away so you can form a right angle. You probably won't be able to do this the first time. Don't force it. Now try to do the same thing between the second and third toes, the third and the fourth and the fourth and the fifth.

You can repeat the procedure on your left foot immediately after, or lie down and compare the two halves of your body.

You can also continue to massage your right foot. Place the palm of your left hand against the sole of the right foot and put your fingers between your toes. Proceed gently again up to the base of the toes and flex the front of the foot toward you until the toe joints appear. Observe the effects of this exercise by getting up and walking lightly.

4. *The back*

Bertherat calls this the "hammock" and recommends it particularly for women who have painful periods. Find a soft ball about the size of a grapefruit. Lie down, legs bent and slightly apart, feet flat on the ground. Try to relax the muscles of the legs, the jaw and the shoulders. Place the ball under the sacrum and the tailbone and stop moving. Let the back take on the shape of a hammock. Relax your stomach. Take the time needed to get the relief needed. Just let go. Now remove the ball and observe the effects on the lower back.

5. *The legs*

This exercise works on the legs. Lie down on the floor, legs bent, feet flat, neck stretched. Take the front part of your right foot in your hand and gently stretch out your right leg sideways and upwards. Keep your spine as flat as possible against the floor, relax your shoulders and leave the right half of the body stretched out. Don't worry about performance but breathe "with" the movement while raising your leg and returning it to its original position. While exhaling, you will make a patient, slow and gradual effort. Then stretch out completely and observe the effects of the exercise. You can also stand up and compare your two legs.

You can now do the same exercise with your left leg or, if you want to, stretch both legs at once.

6. *The shoulders*

Sit down, both feet flat on the ground so that your weight is evenly shared on both buttocks. Put your right hand in the middle of your left shoulder against the skin. Gently but firmly grasp the trapezius muscle with your entire hand. Let the left arm hang. Now raise the left shoulder slowly, then turning from front to back, make circles with the rounding of the shoulder. Hold the trapezius muscle firmly so that it will do as little work as possible and completely relax the left arm. Make one movement per breath. Now to compare the two halves of the body, put your arms down on each side and turn both shoulders simultaneously.

7. Back of the neck

While seated, slowly turn the head to the left, then to the right. Now grasp the muscles at the back of the neck in your hand. Relax your jaws and tongue and nod your head slightly, shake it gently from side to side, then make little circles with the tip of your nose. Breathe normally. Now, let go of your neck and look from left to right to feel the effects of this exercise.

8. The hands, the arms and the face

Find a ball about the size of an orange or just use an orange. Lie down, legs bent so that your middle back is comfortably on the floor, your arms at your sides, palms down and inside thighs relaxed. Place the ball near your right hand. Keeping your shoulder, elbow and forearm on the floor, gently roll the ball with the tips of your fingers toward your feet without losing it, as if your arm were elastic. Then, resting on your elbow with the ball in your palm, raise your hand and forearm upwards with your palm still turned down. Then slowly raise the ball upwards. Stop the movement when your forearm is vertical. Spread your fingers and feel the ball in the hollow of your hand. Continue to breathe normally. Slowly bring your arm and palm against the floor and compare the state of your two arms. This exercise also relaxes facial muscles. Sit up and observe the effects.

9. Breathing

Lie down, legs bent, feet flat on the floor, feet and knees spread to the width of your hips. Put your two hands on your ribcage just above the waist and concentrate on the movements of your breathing. Now fully grasp the skin just at the edge of the last two ribs of the ribcage and lift the skin upwards. Keep the skin lifted while inhaling and exhaling. Don't force the inhalation and exhale quite deeply. Take several breaths.

Now, using both hands again, lift the skin below the ribs and a little above the waist. Repeat the above.

Take a few moments to observe your breathing movements once the exercise is completed.

10. *The pelvis*

Find a sponge ball the size of an orange. Lie down, legs bent. Pay attention to your back, your waist, your shoulder blades. Place the ball in the upper part of your right buttock where the sacral joints meet. Let the weight of your buttock rest on the ball and let the left buttock rest on the floor. Keep your waist as close as possible to the floor. Relax, breathe normally. Slowly bring your right knee up to your chest, being careful to keep the ball in place. Now slowly stretch out your left leg and while continuing to pull your right knee towards your chest, pay attention to the inside of your thighs. Make little circles with the right knee with the help of your right hand. Observe the circles that are being made at the same time in the pelvic area which is resting on the ball. Gently return to your original position by first flexing the right leg, then putting your right foot down flat. Remove the ball and feel the difference in the pelvis. Get up slowly and, while walking, observe the effects of the exercise in one half of your body, from the face to the foot.

RELAXATION BREAKS

Now we will suggest some rapid and easy exercises to be done during an ordinary day. These exercises are a good substitute for a coffee-break. They let you re-centre and re-energize yourself immediately. We will talk about the breathing break, the withdrawal break and the awareness break. There are several other types of breaks and all are effective in reducing tension and fatigue. If your work is intellectual and you work seated, any kind of movement encourages rest : yawning, stirring, stretching or standing up for several moments. If your work demands exercise and muscular strength, sitting or doing nothing becomes an excellent relaxation break.

1. *Breathing break*

Often in our daily routine, we do not breathe at the rate and depth needed to take in all the oxygen we need or to rid the lungs of the stale air that has accumulated. Stress situations cause us to further reduce our respiratory capacity. There is a very strong link between breathing and the energy available to the body. All current psychological theories claim a direct relationship between the quality of breathing and the vitality of the organism. In the fear state, for example, breathing is minimal. On the other hand, in pleasant situations such as making love, we breathe more fully and there is more movement and expression. Chronically deficient respiration leads to increased tension, lack of concentration, and increased anxiety and irritability. Over a long period, this results in constant fatigue and depression.

The breathing break can be taken before, during or after an activity. To get into the habit, it's best to associate it with specific times of the day. Choose some daily activities and plan specific times for breathing breaks: for example, before a class, after a telephone call or during a meal. At the beginning, you will forget a few times but, if you proceed systematically, you will gradually develop the habit of taking a breathing break at those times.

There are many ways to breathe better. We suggest a simple method. First, be sure to take a position that allows you to breathe as deeply as possible. Stand up or lie on a hard surface. If you have to remain seated, lean your back against the back of the chair so that the abdomen can be as mobile as possible. Then concentrate on your breathing without altering its rate or depth. Simply observe the movements of inhaling and exhaling. After a few moments, gradually breathe more deeply. Take several deep breaths without forcing them. With practice, you can set a better breathing rhythm more and more easily.

2. *Withdrawal break*

Dreaming or having your head in the clouds is a withdrawal break that we all practise to some degree. Almost everyone has been distracted in class, for example, by fantasies about vacations or holidays or has missed an important point during a meeting because the mind is wandering.

The withdrawal break we are proposing uses the daydream deliberately for relaxation purposes. Let your mind roam into a fantasy world. This exercise not only lets you release accumulated tension but also identifies the sources of the prevailing tension. If you feel ill at ease with people at a social gathering, you'll undoubtedly imagine a situation where you are alone or with people you like. The daydream is a projection of need. We dream of the people or things we love, we think of a problem to be solved or we think of a happy memory. The daydream indicates the inner need or tension: it is the first step in relaxing.

Here is how the exercise is done.

Be sure you are comfortable and preferably seated. Take the time to take several deep breaths, emptying your lungs as much as possible when exhaling. Close your eyes and let your mind wander. Let yourself be carried away by the images. Go completely into this imaginary world. Take the time needed to see, hear, taste, touch or breathe in the images which come. Then, opening your eyes, get back in touch with the real situation. Give yourself another few moments to feel the relaxed state and compare here and elsewhere. Perhaps you will discover that important needs are unsatisfied or that certain problems are bothering you and taking all your attention. According to Gestalt theory, from the German word meaning "all" or "organized form," unfinished situations exhaust our vital energy by constantly clamoring to be completed or to form good "gestalts." If the daydream lets you see that this is so, plan a time when you can centre all your attention on the problem before going back to your current activity — or do it immediately, if possible. You will be surprised at the energy renewal.

3. *The awareness break*

The awareness break lets you better see who you are and better choose what you want to be to avoid futile sources of tension. It is a retrospective of events in which you simply observe what has happened without censure or evaluation. A moralizing or punitive attitude interferes with this mental process. If you do not have the detachment needed to do this, it would be better not to try.

The awareness break can be taken at any time of the day but the evening is the most opportune time. Choose ten minutes towards the end of the day when you can be alone and quiet. Close your eyes and imagine, as if you were watching a movie, everything that has happened since you got up. You are the director. Take a great many shots from all angles to make the film as meaningful as possible. Watch yourself act, react, feel. Observe your way of talking and thinking as if you were watching an actor on the screen. Note the moments when you were tense and try to understand how the tension developed. Also note the moments when you felt good. Discover the conditions which let that happen, then stop the film and ask yourself if you are satisfied with the scenario. If you could rewrite it, what would you change? How would you like tomorrow's story to unfold? Afterwards, return slowly to your concerns, remembering that you are really the actor, the director and the screenwriter in your life.

15. Emotional control

The rational-emotional strategy is a technique developed by Albert Ellis to fight irrational ideas and alleviate or eradicate certain emotional troubles. Although it requires disciplined, prolonged and persistent work, this technique is very simple. It is especially recommended for stress problems arising from unpleasant emotions such as fear, anxiety, anger or sadness, since it aims at reducing the frequency and intensity of these emotions and increasing the frequency and intensity of pleasant emotions.

To better understand and use this strategy, if needed, let's explain three key concepts : emotion, external event and ideas. Ellis sees emotions as internal events caused by physical stimulation (e.g., a handshake makes you feel good), sensory motor process (e.g., city noise causes negative feelings) or the processes of thought or desire (e.g., the idea of doing your income-tax return depresses you.).

There are three possible ways to control unpleasant emotions : using physical methods such as drugs, medications or alcohol, acting on the sensory motor system through yoga, relaxation, etc., or changing your way of thinking. According to this approach, the first two ways do not bring about lasting well-being so modifying one's way of thinking is the favored method.

People generally believe that their emotions are caused by external events. We frequently hear that failing an exam is depressing or losing a job is catastrophic. We see emotions as inevitable consequences of external events which are the cause of our emotional state.

Let's take an example. You find a parking ticket on your windshield and you get angry. If someone asks you why you are angry, you'll probably say because of the ticket. However, a week later, the same thing happens and this time you laugh at your own negligence because that day you successfully completed a difficult job.

Thus the external event is not the cause of the emotion we feel since, in the same type of situation, our reactions differ from one time to the other. We perceive external events through a highly subjective screen of analysis and interpretation, which is why our reactions vary.

Our assessment or perception of an event is often summed up in the form of sentences that we mentally repeat to ourselves during the day. Observe your thoughts when you are alone and you will easily see this inner monologue.

These sentences are often the direct cause of our emotions, since they sum up our perceptions or assessments of reality or they are linked to our emotional states and influence them. Faced with a difficult job, your emotions can be negative or positive: in one case, you may tell yourself you'll never finish and, in the other, you may feel it is an interesting challenge. It is difficult, in practice, to distinguish between thought and emotion and, obviously, behavior: positive thoughts are associated with positive emotions and behavior, and negative thoughts are associated with negative emotions and behavior.

The ideas which cause unpleasant emotions are often irrational ideas about oneself, others or the world. For example, many people feel that everyone should love them for everything they do or they believe they should succeed in everything they undertake. Others believe the opposite: their characters are basically bad or neurotic which leads to feeling they deserve blame, punishment or rejection.

Irrational ideas can be about people around us. For example, we can think that other people are awful or wonderful, that they do things purposely to hurt us or that it's their fault if we are sad, angry or miserable.

Life or events can also be the subject of irrational ideas. Life should be easy, calm, foreseeable. Things should be the way we want them, whether it be an apartment, a meal, a car or a workplace.

The emotional problems these irrational ideas can cause are easy to imagine. Indeed, as reality rarely corresponds to our wishes and ideals, we can easily feel angry, sad, disappointed or bewildered when differences occur between our desires and reality.

The rational-emotional strategy proposes an attack on irrational ideas and their validity in order to gradually substitute more realistic ideas, if necessary.

For example, when a co-worker refuses your invitation and you think, "I'm not interesting enough for him," you could ask yourself, "Does his refusal necessarily mean that I am not interesting? Doesn't he have the right to choose the women he feels good with? Why should everyone like me? Is this refusal really catastrophic?" These questions will undoubtedly make you think more realistically. You could tell yourself that refusals are unpleasant but you can certainly live with them; also, they do not mean you are uninteresting.

Let's sum up the important points of the rational-emotional strategy, using the following illustration. When an event (A) brings about disagreeable emotional and behavioral consequences (C), the direct "cause" of the disturbance felt is located in the beliefs and ideas (B) that we have about this event.

RATIONAL-EMOTIONAL STRATEGY

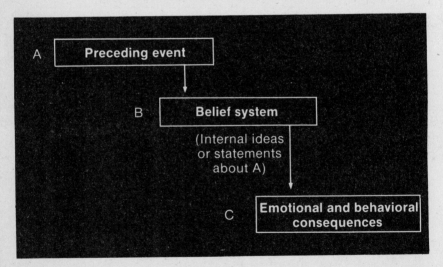

Since the source of the emotions is not in the external events but in the ideas we form about these events, we can effectively control the unpleasant emotions by attacking these ideas. The combat takes the form of a mental debate where irrational ideas are questioned and replaced, if necessary, by more realistic ideas.

Let's explain the procedure, step by step:

1. When you feel an unpleasant emotion, get used to going back to the source of this feeling and identifying the event which set it off. Even though you may find this difficult at the beginning, in time you will be able to do it more and more quickly.

2. Identify the ideas you had at the moment or you still have when you think about the event. Note your inner monologue. Watch out for verbs like "should" or "must", adverbs like "always" or "never" and adjectives like "terrible", "catastrophic" or "dreadful". These words are often indicative of irrational ideas.

3. Question and debate the irrational idea. You will be able to see, through changes in feeling or behavior, if you have succeeded at this or not. Obviously, things will not change drastically from one day to the next. Continue the inner debate as long as necessary.

4. a) If you see that your ideas are realistic and your disturbance is well-founded, try to change the event which causes the disturbance. If no action is impossible, tell yourself to be patient and avoid amplifying or distorting your disturbance.

b) If you see that your ideas are irrational, replace them with realistic ideas.

Let's take an example:

1. You've felt depressed since yesterday. You think of your last meeting with Anne. She hasn't shown much feeling for you for a while. She is cool and distant. You've asked her about it, but she doesn't want to discuss it for the moment.

2. Little by little, identify the ideas in your mind at the time of the incident: "Perhaps she no longer loves me? Perhaps she's angry. It would be terrible if she no longer loved me! Life is unfair!" Note the key words: here are unrealistic ideas which cause unpleasant emotions.

3. Take a few minutes to debate these ideas. Does Anne's being distant necessarily mean she no longer loves you? Couldn't she be preoccupied, tired or just want to be alone? Does loving someone mean you have to feel in love all day long? And if she no longer loves you, would it really be catastrophic? Couldn't you face this? Is life unfair because of this? In this questioning, you will gradually come to refute your unrealistic ideas and replace them with thoughts like these: "It's not certain she no longer loves me and, even if she doesn't, I won't die; I'll be sad but that doesn't make life unfair; loving involves risks and I can handle a break-up and go on living without this girl." Because your friend doesn't want to talk about it now, tell yourself to be patient until the situation has been clarified and each time irrational ideas come into your mind, substitute more realistic thoughts and occupy yourself with other things to avoid increasing your disturbance.

Stress, as we have seen, depends on subjective evaluation of danger. Perception and stress are linked phenomena. Since the rational-emotional strategy lets us alter our perceptions, it can help us assess danger realistically and reduce the stress caused by prejudices or irrational ideas. The more you realize the number of problems created this way, the more you will see that the rational-emotional strategy is a highly useful discipline.

CONCLUSION

Stress cannot be avoided; it is inevitable. But as we have seen, it can cost a lot. Each time the body reacts to a stressor, numerous biochemical changes occur and, if the stressor goes beyond the available adaptive abilities, illness or even death can result.

Rather than battling against stress, try to optimize the stress in your life: adopt a lifestyle that is stimulating but serene and maintain a physical and mental state which gives you increased resistance to stressors. It's not a matter of fighting stress but of managing your life.

If you have followed this guide, you have defined the stress in your life, examined different solutions and opted for one of them. You have planned an action strategy and applied it. And now? As in all problem-solving processes, the results of your action must be evaluated in terms of the objective sought; you must observe the faults in the process and more accurately measure the difficulty of change and understand the situation from the experience you have gained. Are you satisfied with the results? Do you want to make other changes? How does the problem appear now? After the evaluation, is another problem-solving process necessary? You now have the knowledge and skills you need. It's up to you to use them.

Bibliography

ANDREASEN, N.J.C., RUSSELL, Noyes, Jr., HARTFORD, C.E. Factors influencing adjustment of burn patients during hospitalization. *Psychosomatic Medecine*, 34, 517-523, 1972.

APPLEY, M.H., TRUMBULL, R. On the concept of psychological stress. *Psychological Stress: Issues In Research*. Englewood Cliffs, New Jersey: Prentice-Hall, 1967.

ABRAHAMSON, E.M., PEZET, A.W. *Body, mind and sugar*. New York: Avon Books, 1951.

AUGER, L. *S'aider soi-même*. Montréal: Éditions de l'Homme. Éditions du CIM, 1974.

Aviation Royale du Canada (ed.). *Le programme 5BX*. Ottawa: Ministère de la défense nationale, 1964.

Aviation Royale du Canada (ed.). *Le programme 10BX*. Ottawa: Ministère de la défense nationale, 1964.

BATESON, G. *Steps to an ecology of mind*. New York: Ballantine Books, 1972.

BERTHERAT, Thérèse. *Le corps a ses raisons*. Paris: Éditions du Seuil, 1976.

BOUCHARD, C., LANDRY, F., BRUNELLE, J., GODBOUT, P. *La condition physique et le bien-être*. Québec: Éditions du Pélican, 1974.

BOUCHER, Francine, AVARD, Jacqueline. *Méthodes d'études et efficacité personnelle*. Montréal: Les Publications du Service d'Orientation et de Consultation Psychologique de l'Université de Montréal (à venir).

BOUCHER, P. L'euphorie se meurt... vive l'eustress. *Les Cahiers du Psychologue Québécois*, 1, n° 7, 1979.

BRUNET, J.M. *Vivez en santé: vivez heureux*. Montréal: Québécor, 1978.

CANNON, W.B. «"Voodoo" death». *American Anthropologist*, 44, 169-181, 1942.

CHERASKIN, E. Ringsdorf, W.M. *Psycho-dietetics*. New-York: Bantam Books, 1974.

186

COOPER, K.H. *The Aerobics way*. New York: M. Evans, 1977.

CULLIGAN, M.J., SEDLACEK, Keith. *How to kill stress before it kills you*. New York: Grosset and Dunlap, 1976.

DE LAUNIÈRE, C., GAGNON, Pauline. Un marketing transcendental. *Québec Science*, **17**, n° 4, 1978.

DAVIS, J.T. *Walking*! New York: Bantam Books, 1979.

DOHRENWEND, B., DOHRENWEND B. (ed.). *Stress fuel life events; their nature and effects*: New York: Wiley and Sons, 1974.

DUFTY, W. *Sugar blues*. New York: Warner Books, 1976.

DUNBAR, F. *Psychosomatic diagnosis*. New York: Harper, 1943.

ELLIS, A. *Humanistic psychotherapy: the rational-emotive approach*. New York: Julian Press, 1973.

ELLIS, A., GRIEGER, R. *Handbook of rational-emotive therapy*. New York: Springer, 1977.

ELLIS, A., HARPER, R.A. *A guide to rational living*. Englewood Cliffs: Prentice-Hall, 1961.

EPSTEIN, S. Anxiety, arousal and the self-concept. *In* Sarason, I. G., Spielberger, C.D. (ed.). *Stress and anxiety*. (vol. 3). New York: John Wiley and Sons, 1976.

ESCOFFIER-LAMBIOTTE. Une découverte majeure en France sur l'hypertension. *Le Devoir*, 20 mars, p. 8, 1979.

FIXX, J.F. *The complete book of running*. New York: Random House, 1977.

FREDERICKS, C. *Psycho-nutrition*. New York: Grosset and Dunlap, 1976.

FRIED, M. Grieving for a lost home *in* Dulh, L.J. (ed.). *The urban condition: people and policy, in the metropolis*. New York: Basic Books, 1963.

FRIEDMAN, M., ROSENMAN, R.H. *Type A behavior and your heart*. New York: Alfred A. Knopf, 1974.

FRIEDMAN, S.B., CHODOFF, P., MASON, J.W., HAMBURG, D.A. Behavioral observations on parents anticipating the death of a child. *Pediatrics*, **32**, 610–625, 1963.

GLASS, D.C., SINGER, J.E. *Urban stress: experiments on noise and social stressors*. New York: Academic Press, 1972.

GLASSER, W. *Positive addiction*. New York: Harper and Row, 1976.

HACKETT, T.P., WEISMAN, A.D. Reactions to the imminence of death, *in* Grosser, G.H. *et al.* (ed.). *The threat of impending disasters*. Cambridge: MIT Press, 1964.

HAY, D., OKEN, D. The psychological stress of intensive care unit nursing. *Psychosomatic Medecine*, **34**, 109–118, 1972.

HENDERSON, J. *Jog, run, race*. Mountain view, California: World Publications, 1977.

HOLMES, T.H., RAHE, R.H. The social readjustment rating scale. *Journal of Psychosomatic Research*, **11**, 1967.

JACOB, R. Travail et stress: l'urgence d'agir. *Les Cahiers du Psychologue Québécois*, 1979.

JACOBSON, M.F. *Nutrition scoreboard*. New York: Avon Books, 1974.

JACOBSON, E. *You must relax*. New York: McGraw-Hill, 1962.

JANIS, I.L. *Stress and frustration*. New York: Harcourt Brace Javanovich Inc., 1969.

KAHN, R.C. *et al. Organizational stress: studies in role conflict and ambiguity*. New York: Wiley, 1964.

KATZ, J.L., WEINER, H., GALLAGHER, T.F. HELLMAN, L. Stress, distress and ego defenses. *Archives of General Psychiatry*, **23**, 131–142, 1970.

LAING, R.D. *The divided self*. Harmondsworth: Penguin Books, 1959.

LAKEIN, A. *How to get control of your time and your life*. New York: Peter H. Wyden Inc., 1973.

LAZARUS, R.S. Psychological stress and coping in adaptation and illness. *International Journal of Psychiatry in Medecine*, **5**, 321–333, 1974 b.

LE SHAN, L. *How to meditate*. Boston: Bantam, 1974.

LIEF, H.I., FOX, R.S. Training for « detached concern » in medical students, in Lief, H.I. *et al.* (ed.). *The psychological basis of medical practice*, New York: Harper and Row, 1963.

LINDEMANN, E. Symptomatology and management of acute grief. *American Journal of Psychiatry*, **101**, 141–148, 1944.

MACKENZIE, R.A. *The time trap*. New York: Amacom, 1972.

MAHONEY, M.J. *Self-change: strategies for solving personal problems*. New York: W.N. Norton and Co., 1979.

MARLATT, G.A. Alcohol, stress and cognitive control, *in* Sarason, I.G., Spielberger, C.D. (ed.). *Stress and anxiety*. (vol. 3). New York: John Wiley and Sons, 1976.

MASON, J.W. A re-evaluation of the concept of non-specificity in stress theory. *Journal of Psychiatric Research*, **8**, 323-333, 1971.

MASON, J.W. A historical view of the stress field: part 1. *Journal of Human Stress*, **1**, 6-12, 1975 a.

MASON, J.W. A historical view of the stress field: part 2. *Journal of Human Stress*, **1**, 22-36, 1975 b.

MCGRATH, J.E. Settings, measures and themes: an integrative view of some research on social-psychological factors in stress, *in* McGrath, J.E. (ed.). *Social and psychological factors in stress*. New York: Holt, Rinehart and Winston, 1970.

MCLEAN, P.D. Depression as a specific response to stress, *in* Sarason, I.G., Spielberger, C.D. (ed.). *Stress and anxiety*. (vol. 3). New York: John Wiley and Sons, 1976.

MCQUADE, W., Aikman, Ann. *Stress*. New York: Bantam, 1974.

MECHANIC, D. *Students under stress: a study in the social psychology of adaptation*. New York: The Free Press, 1962.

MENNINGER, K. Regulatory device of the ego under major stress. *International Journal of Psychoanalysis*, **35**, 412-420, 1954.

Ministère des Affaires Sociales. *Une politique québécoise en matière de nutrition*. Québec, 1977.

Ministère des Affaires Sociales. *Guide alimentaire québécois*. Québec, 1979.

Ministère de la Santé et du Bien-être Social. *Rapport sur les habitudes alimentaires*. Ottawa, 1975.

Ministère de la Santé et du Bien-être social. *Le manuel du guide alimentaire canadien*. Ottawa, 1977.

MOREHOUSE, L.E., GROSS, L. *Maximum performance*. New York: Pocket Book, 1977.

MOREHOUSE, L.E., Gross, L. *Total fitness in thirty minutes a week*. New York: Hart-Davis, 1976.

MURRAY, A. *Modern weight training*. Londres: Kaye and Ward, 1971.

O.P.T.A.T. (ed.). *Phénomène drogue*. Québec: O.P.T.A.T., 1973.

PALM, J.D. *Diet away your stress, tension and anxiety*. New York: Pocket Books, 1977.

PICARD, F. Toxicomanies: une consommation à la hausse. *Québec Science. 17*, n° 4, p. 51, 1978.

RAHE, R.H., RANSOM, J.A. Life-change patterns surrounding illness. *Journal of Psychosomatic Research, 11*, 341–345, 1968.

SCHAFER, W. *Stress, distress and growth*. Davis, California: Responsible Action, 1978.

SELYE, H. *Stress sans détresse*. Montréal: La Presse, 1974.

SHAPIRO, D. *Nevrotic styles*. New York: Basic Books, 1965.

SHARPE, R., LEWIS, D. *Thrive on stress. How to make it to your advantage*. New York: Warner Books, 1978.

SPIRO, M.E. Religious systems as culturally constituted defense mechanisms, *in Content and meaning in cultural anthropology*. New York: The Free Press, 1965.

TANNER, O. *Le stress*. New York: Time Life Books, 1976.

TOFFLER, A. *Future shock*. New York: Bantam Books, 1970.

WATSON, D.L., THARP, R.E. *Self-directed behavior*. Monterey: Brooks/Cole Publishing Co., 1977.

WATZLAWICK, P., WEAKLAND, V., FISCH, R. *Change*. New York: W.W. Norton and Co., 1974.

WHELAN, Élisabeth M., STARE, F.J. *Panic in the pantry*. New York: Atheneum, 1977.

WHITTLESEY, Marietta. *Killer salt*. New York: Avon Books, 1978.

WOLFF, H.G. *Stress and disease*. Springfield, Illinois: Charles C. Thomas, 1968.

ZBOROWSKI, M. *People in pain*. Boston: Jossey-Bass Inc., 1969.